Great
Main Dishes

Great
Main Dishes

Robert Carrier

Angus & Robertson Publishers

Photographs in this series taken by Christian Délu, John Miller, Jack Nisberg, Iain Reid, Pipe-Rich
Design by Martin Atcherley for The Nassington Press Ltd.
Line drawings by Sally Launder

Some material in this book has already been published in
The Robert Carrier Cookbook
Published in 1965 by
Thomas Nelson and Sons Ltd.
© Copyright Robert Carrier 1965

ANGUS & ROBERTSON PUBLISHERS
London . Sydney . Melbourne . Singapore
Manila

First published in Australia by Angus & Robertson Publishers, Australia, 1979

© Robert Carrier 1978

National Library of Australia
Cataloguing-in-publication data.

Carrier, Robert
  Great main dishes.

  Index
  ISBN 0 207 14240 8 Hardbound
  ISBN 0 207 14184 3 Paperbound

  1. Cookery. I. Title.
641.82

Printed in Singapore

Contents

Useful Facts and Figures

Notes on metrication

When making any of the recipes in this book, only follow one set of measures as they are not interchangeable.

In this book quantities are given in metric and Imperial measures. Exact conversion from Imperial to metric measures does not usually give very convenient working quantities and so the metric measures have been rounded off into units of 25 grams. The table below shows the recommended equivalents.

Ounces	Approx gram to nearest whole figure	Recommended conversion to nearest unit of 25
1	28	25
2	57	50
3	85	75
4	113	100
5	142	150
6	170	175
7	198	200
8	227	225
9	255	250
10	283	275
11	312	300
12	340	350
13	368	375
14	396	400
15	425	425
16 (1 lb)	454	450
17	482	475
18	510	500
19	539	550
20 (1¼ lb)	567	575

Note: When converting quantities over 20 oz first add the appropriate figures in the centre column, then adjust to the nearest unit of 25. As a general guide, 1 kg (1000 g) equals 2.2 lb or about 2 lb 3 oz. This method of conversion gives good results in nearly all cases, although in certain pastry and cake recipes a more accurate conversion is necessary to produce a balanced recipe.

Liquid measures

The millilitre has been used in this book and the following table gives a few examples.

Imperial	Approx ml to nearest whole figure	Recommended ml
¼ pint	142	150 ml
½ pint	283	300 ml
¾ pint	425	450 ml
1 pint	567	600 ml
1½ pints	851	900 ml
1¾ pints	992	1000 ml (1 litre)

Can sizes

At present, cans are marked with the exact (usually to the nearest whole number) metric equivalent of the Imperial weight of the contents, so we have followed this practice when giving can sizes.

Oven temperatures

The table below gives recommended equivalents.

	°C	°F	Gas Mark
Very cool	110	225	$\frac{1}{4}$
	120	250	$\frac{1}{2}$
Cool	140	275	1
	150	300	2
Moderate	160	325	3
	180	350	4
Moderately hot	190	375	5
	200	400	6
Hot	220	425	7
	230	450	8
Very hot	240	475	9

Notes for American and Australian users

In America the 8-oz measuring cup is used. In Australia metric measures are now used in conjunction with the standard 250-ml measuring cup. The Imperial pint, used in Britain and Australia, is 20 fl oz, while the American pint is 16 fl oz. It is important to remember that the Australian tablespoon differs from both the British and American tablespoons; the table below gives a comparison. The British standard tablespoon, which has been used throughout this book, holds 17.7 ml, the American 14.2 ml, and the Australian 20 ml. A teaspoon holds approximately 5 ml in all three countries.

British	American	Australian
1 teaspoon	1 teaspoon	1 teaspoon
1 tablespoon	1 tablespoon	1 tablespoon
2 tablespoons	3 tablespoons	2 tablespoons
$3\frac{1}{2}$ tablespoons	4 tablespoons	3 tablespoons
4 tablespoons	5 tablespoons	$3\frac{1}{2}$ tablespoons

An Imperial/American guide to solid and liquid measures

Solid measures

Imperial	American
1 lb butter or margarine	2 cups
1 lb flour	4 cups
1 lb granulated or castor sugar	2 cups
1 lb icing sugar	3 cups
8 oz rice	1 cup

Liquid measures

Imperial	American
$\frac{1}{4}$ pint liquid	$\frac{2}{3}$ cup liquid
$\frac{1}{2}$ pint	$1\frac{1}{4}$ cups
$\frac{3}{4}$ pint	2 cups
1 pint	$2\frac{1}{2}$ cups
$1\frac{1}{2}$ pints	$3\frac{3}{4}$ cups
2 pints	5 cups ($2\frac{1}{2}$ pints)

Introduction

'In this competitive age,' wrote William Makepeace Thackeray in the last century, 'hospitality is being pressed into service and becoming an excuse for ostentation. Dinners are given mostly by way of revenge.'

The climax to this unhappy state of affairs was reached in America in the Gay Nineties, when a famous socialite decided to make her first big splash in Washington society. Abashed by rival political hostesses' habits of enfolding a costly jewelled or gold trinket in each guest's napkin, she decided that there was only one way to beat them at their own game. When her turn came to give a large dinner party, she wrapped a crisp new one hundred dollar bill in the napkin at each plate!

But the new trend in entertaining is away from big parties. The famous American publisher who had three guest lists for his equally famous parties – the 'A' list for Society; the 'B' list made up of actors, writers and other celebrities; and the 'C' list, a sort of catch-all for wits, favourite beauties and close friends – is a glamorous figure from a dead, dead past.

Small gatherings where everyone gets a chance to talk to everyone else are the new rule; intimate suppers for four, dinner parties for six to eight, country luncheons for eight to ten, buffet parties and after-theatre parties for eight to twenty. The result: a more friendly feeling, and conversation of a more thoughtful and informed calibre – except, of course, at the parties of the younger, cool set, where everyone sits on the floor and listens to records hour after hour, or at cocktail parties, where the talk is as impossible and improbable as it ever used to be. But one thing is true of today's parties: food is uppermost – everyone eats!

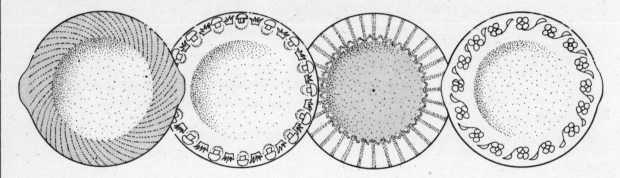

While some well-known hostesses explode like Roman candles with gimmicky party ideas to dazzle their guests, I much prefer the warm candlelight technique of the hostess who sees to every need but wastes no time on glittering pyrotechnics. Good seating, good food, good conversation: what more can anyone ask?

Well, I can tell you that asking your guests to 'come as you are' or 'as the person you hate' can backfire, and you may find that you are the one they hate most for such scandalous trickery. Entertaining, when properly done, needs no gimmicks. Try and mix people of all kinds and varieties at your parties – whether you are the guiding light behind a charity ball, tossing an after-theatre buffet at home, a highly perfected picnic in the country, or a dazzling dinner in town.

And give them something different. If you are entertaining visiting Americans, for instance, do not fall into the trap of giving them baked Virginia ham and candied sweet potatoes with marshmallows. Far better to lead them down the English byways of Star Gazey pie, Lancashire hotpot and old-fashioned treacle tart. The last thing in the world you want is to make visitors feel as though they were back at home. Far better that they should stagger about discussing the wonders of British cookery than merely observing that the English can turn out a damned fine hamburger!

To entertain with ease means planning as much do-it-ahead preparation as possible either in the morning or preferably the day before, so that you can then forget you are the host or hostess and just have fun.

Develop a repertoire of dishes that you do especially well and feel at ease in preparing. And then add a few new specialities to this list each year.

Do keep a record of the parties you give and the guests who attend each one. There is nothing worse for a guest than being served **paella** (no matter how delicious) every time he comes. In this way you can be sure you will not repeat your menus and serve the same people the same dishes each and every time.

If you are planning a new dish which sounds fabulous, try it out on the family or one or two close friends first. This gives you a chance to check on ingredients and on cooking times . . . and what is more important, allows you to add your own special touch to make the recipe more personally yours.

And remember, the true art of entertaining comes from knowing and being yourself. Do not struggle with a six-course dinner when informal casseroles are your *forte*. Being yourself means living by your own standards, not those of others. You can find fascinating ways, well within the scope of your own limitations, to entertain anyone, from a visiting diplomat to a visiting member of the family, without trying to do what is 'expected'.

A dinner party in Cannes, given one summer by the famous French *antiquaires* Grognot and Joinel in their luxury summer apartment overlooking the Old Port of Cannes, taught me what true simplicity can be. Four courses, if you count the gloriously simple green salad, made up this meal . . . and the only wine served with it was Sancerre, a *vin nouveau*, the perfect accompaniment. The first course was **rougets à la niçoise**, a dish of lightly grilled red mullet, followed by **poulet au blanc**, a tender chicken cooked in cream in the manner of Mère Blanc, well-known restaurant owner of Vonnas. A green salad with herbs and a **salade des fruits** completed this delicious meal. When one thinks of entertaining in terms as simple as these, it becomes more of a pleasure.

Entertaining in our day is so much easier than it was in Edwardian times. Of course, you may not have the scores of domestic servants that some families enjoyed in those days, but neither do you have twenty people sitting down for Sunday lunch, and your dinners do not have to go on for course after heavy course of complicated foods to keep up with the Joneses. Nor do you have to go twice a year to Baden-Baden to recover from these excesses. Today we have our electric equipment, the know-how of modern refrigeration, science and merchandising . . . and we have our four-course dinner with the continentally inspired casserole as star performer.

Although I entertain frequently, I like my parties to be simple and intimate, in keeping with the kind of life I live. Never any fussy cocktail bits with the drinks, but, for special occasions, bacon-wrapped prawns, prunes or chicken livers served hot, tiny *brioches* filled with *foie gras,* or iced celery stuffed with caviar and cream cheese – or no cocktail food at all but quantities of good food after: practically never more than four courses at any dinner party, but each course substantial and interesting in itself.

Two words of warning for the unwary: be realistic about your budget and stay within bounds. And stick to a dish you know you can do successfully with no last-minute grilling or warming up while your guests sit fidgeting at the table.

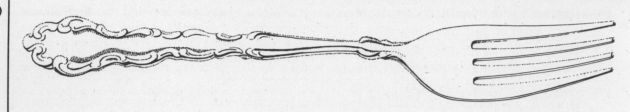

Choosing Your Menu

The conventional opening for a formal dinner has always been clear soup, followed by fish, an entrée and a pudding. But why be conventional? There are no longer any rules for this sort of thing. I much prefer a memorable dish such as **crêpes aux sardines,** a recipe brought back by the hostess from a holiday on the Basque coast – served with imagination and pride – to all the clear soups in the world. I shall always remember those *crêpes,* crisply golden, with their delicately blended filling of fresh sardines, pounded over ice and mixed (like *quenelles*) with whipped cream and egg white, and indeed, I have since served them (the sincerest form of flattery) at my own dinners. The *crêpes* were followed by **poulet à la basquaise,** chicken in a white wine sauce, served with baked green peppers stuffed with saffron rice.

So be adventurous and try new ways with old favourites – serve cold lamb with *mayonnaise comme au Pay des Landes*, creamy mayonnaise lightly flavoured with garlic; try the humble mussel, skewered *en brochette* with alternate slices of bacon, the whole rolled in flour, egg yolk and breadcrumbs, deep-fried in golden oil and served with sauce Béarnaise; or slit 'pockets' in thick lamb chops and stuff them with savoury garlic and herb butter. Delicious!

Serve a fillet of beef *en croûte*, but first cut your fillet into thick serving pieces; spread each slice with a paste of finely chopped mushrooms and onion which you have sautéed in butter until soft, and insert a slice of cooked ham or boiled bacon between each slice. This is skewered together and roasted in the usual way before being wrapped in its envelope of puff pastry and baked to golden perfection. It is as delicious cold as it is hot and makes an excellent buffet party dish as well. And for a gala party with no holds barred, precede this dish with salmon soufflé mousse with a prawn and lobster sauce. The mousse – a *quenelle*-like mixture – can be prepared in individual soufflé dishes or in one large ovenproof dish. Sometimes I turn it out just before serving and cover it with its sauce; at other times I serve it in the dish it was baked in, with the sauce passed separately. Either way it is a most attractive first course.

Your menu depends to some extent, of course, on the amount of time you have for preparation and on the time it takes to gather your guests to the table. I like to plan all dinner parties so that nothing, absolutely nothing, will spoil if kept waiting.

If guests are apt to be a little late, it is a good idea to copy the Russian *zakouski* table, set up in a room adjoining the drawing-room and wheeled in. I find this an easy and rather stimulating way to soften the cares of service, and often produce *hors-d'oeuvre*, both hot and cold in the Russian manner, in the drawing-room before going in to dinner, where a hot meat dish – or a hot fish dish followed by cold meats and salad – awaits the guests.

The meal can start in this way with, instead of soup, something which requires absolutely no preparation: the thinnest slices of smoked salmon served with fresh wedges of lemon on an oiled platter, or rolled (budget notwithstanding) around sombre cargoes of Russian caviar; smoked eels or sturgeon, served on beds of chopped ice; and firm pink slices of tongue and ham with olives. Perhaps greenhouse cucumbers, marinated in a soured cream and chives dressing, could bring a touch of early spring to your menu.

Fish

Marinated Cod Steaks

4 slices fresh cod, about 2.5 cm/1 inch thick
butter
onion
175-200 ml/6-7 fl oz canned clam juice or
    well-flavoured fish stock
salt and freshly ground black pepper
4 large potatoes, peeled

SAUCE
2 level tablespoons butter
2 level tablespoons flour
150 ml/¼ pint canned clam juice, or well-
    flavoured fish stock
salt
cayenne
1 egg yolk
150 ml/¼ pint double cream
juice of ¼ lemon

GARNISH
8 heart-shaped croûtons
4 rashers grilled bacon
2 level tablespoons finely chopped parsley

MARINADE 1
olive oil
dry white wine
finely chopped garlic
finely chopped parsley
1 bay leaf, crumbled
salt and freshly ground black pepper

MARINADE 2
1 onion, thinly sliced
½ lemon, thinly sliced
2-3 level tablespoons chopped parsley
1 bay leaf, crumbled
1 level teaspoon peppercorns
½ level teaspoon thyme
½ level teaspoon allspice
3 tablespoons vinegar
1 level tablespoon salt
300 ml/½ pint water

To make marinade 1: combine equal parts olive oil and dry white wine, flavoured with finely chopped garlic and parsley, crumbled bay leaf, salt and freshly ground black pepper, to taste.

To make marinade 2: combine sliced onion, sliced lemon, chopped parsley, crumbled bay leaf, peppercorns, thyme, allspice, vinegar, salt and water in a porcelain bowl.

1. Marinate cod slices for at least 4 hours in marinade 1 or 2.

2. Place marinated cod steaks in a well-buttered *gratin* dish with 1 tablespoon finely chopped onion and 2 to 4 tablespoons of the clam juice: place in double steamer, cover and steam until tender – 10 to 15 minutes. Or place in a saucepan on a bed of sliced onion with 125 ml/¼ pint clam juice, or fish stock, and just enough water to cover fish. Season to taste with salt and freshly ground black pepper. Cover pan and bring to the boil, lower heat and simmer gently for 15 to 20 minutes, until fish flakes easily with a fork.

3. Scoop balls from potatoes with a potato scoop or melon baller. Boil them in salted water for 15 minutes. Drain and reserve.

4. **To make sauce:** heat butter in the top of a double saucepan, add flour and cook over water, stirring, until sauce is smooth and thick. Add canned clam juice and strained pan juices from fish. Season to taste with salt and cayenne, and simmer until smooth. Stir in egg yolk, cream and lemon juice, and simmer until thickened, being careful not to let sauce come to the boil. Strain through a fine sieve into a clean saucepan. Add potato balls to sauce and heat for 3 minutes, stirring from time to time.

5. **To serve:** place fish on a heated serving dish, garnish with *croûtons*, grilled bacon and finely chopped parsley, and serve accompanied by sauce.

Marinated Salmon Steaks *Serves 4*
Grilled Herrings with Mustard *Serves 4*
Grilled Sea Bass aux Herbes *Serves 4 to 6*
Oven Fried Plaice à la Niçoise *Serves 4 to 6*

12

Marinated Salmon Steaks

4 fresh salmon steaks
50 g/2 oz butter
salt and freshly ground black pepper
paprika
2 level tablespoons dried breadcrumbs

MARINADE
1 Spanish onion, sliced
2 cloves garlic, finely chopped
2 sticks celery, sliced
2 bay leaves
4 tablespoons red wine vinegar
4 tablespoons olive oil
4 peppercorns

1. **To make marinade:** combine sliced onion, finely chopped garlic, sliced celery, bay leaves, red wine vinegar, olive oil and peppercorns in a large bowl.

2. Place salmon steaks in the marinade mixture and marinate for at least 2 hours.

3. Remove steaks from marinade, drain and place in a well-buttered ovenproof *gratin* dish. Brush with melted butter and sprinkle with salt, freshly ground black pepper and paprika. Sprinkle lightly with breadcrumbs, place under a preheated grill and grill for 5 minutes. Then bake in a moderate oven (160°C, 325°F, Gas Mark 3) for 5 to 10 minutes longer, until fish flakes easily with a fork.

Grilled Herrings with Mustard

4 fresh herrings
2-3 level tablespoons flour
salt and freshly ground black pepper
olive oil
French mustard
fresh breadcrumbs
4 tablespoons melted butter
boiled new potatoes

1. Clean and scale fresh herrings, taking care not to break the skin underneath. Cut off heads, wash and dry fish carefully.

2. Make 3 shallow incisions on sides of each fish with a sharp knife. Dip herrings in seasoned flour and brush them with olive oil. Grill on a well-oiled baking sheet for 3 to 4 minutes on each side.

3. Arrange herrings in a shallow ovenproof *gratin* dish and brush them liberally with French mustard. Sprinkle with fresh breadcrumbs and melted butter, and put in a very hot oven (240°C, 475°F, Gas Mark 9) for 5 minutes. Serve in the *gratin* dish with boiled new potatoes.

Grilled Sea Bass aux Herbes
Illustrated on page 25

2 sea bass, cleaned
4 level tablespoons flour
olive oil
salt and freshly ground black pepper
2 sprigs each rosemary, fennel, parsley and
   thyme

1. Flour cleaned fish lightly and brush with olive oil. Season generously with salt and freshly ground black pepper.

2. Stuff cavities of fish with fresh herbs and grill for 3 to 5 minutes on each side, until fish flakes easily, basting fish with olive oil from time to time.

Oven Fried Plaice à la Niçoise

4-6 plaice, filleted
1 level tablespoon salt
300 ml/½ pint milk
100 g/4 oz dried breadcrumbs
4 level tablespoons finely chopped parsley
2 cloves garlic, finely chopped
freshly grated peel of ½ lemon
¼ level teaspoon dried thyme
4 tablespoons melted butter
paprika
lemon wedges

1. Add salt to the milk. Dip plaice fillets in the milk and then in the breadcrumbs, which you have mixed with finely chopped parsley, garlic, grated lemon peel and thyme.

2. Arrange the fish pieces in a well-buttered baking dish and pour the melted butter over them. Place the dish on the top shelf of a hot oven (230°C, 450°F, Gas Mark 8) for about 12 minutes. Sprinkle with paprika. Serve with lemon wedges.

Fish Souvlakia

Illustrated on page 28

1 kg/2 lb fresh halibut, haddock or turbot
4 tomatoes, thinly sliced
2 onions, thinly sliced
Rice Pilaff (see below)

MARINADE SAUCE
6 tablespoons olive oil
6 tablespoons dry white wine
1-2 cloves garlic, finely chopped
½ onion, finely chopped
4 level tablespoons finely chopped parsley
1 level teaspoon oregano
salt and freshly ground black pepper

1. Combine Marinade Sauce ingredients in a mixing bowl. Cut fish into 3.5-cm/1½-inch squares and toss in marinade mixture to make sure each piece of fish is properly covered with marinade.

2. Place sliced tomatoes and onion on top of fish and cover bowl with a plate and refrigerate for at least 6 hours. Turn fish several times during marinating period.

3. When ready to cook, place fish on skewers alternating with tomato and onion slices. Dribble Marinade Sauce over fish and vegetables and cook over charcoal or under grill of your cooker until done. Turn skewers frequently, basting several times during cooking. Serve *souvlakia* with Rice Pilaff.

Rice Pilaff

13

350 g/12 oz long-grain rice
½ Spanish onion, finely chopped
butter
450 ml/¾ pint well-flavoured stock
thyme
salt and freshly ground black pepper

1. Wash rice; drain and dry with a cloth.

2. Sauté finely chopped onion in 4 tablespoons butter until a light golden colour. Add rice and continue to cook, stirring constantly, until it begins to take on colour.

3. Pour in hot stock, and season to taste with thyme, salt and freshly ground black pepper. Cover saucepan and place in a moderate oven (180°C, 350°F, Gas Mark 4) for 15 to 20 minutes, until the liquid has been absorbed and the rice is tender but not mushy. Serve with additional butter.

14

Baked Fresh Haddock

1 small fresh haddock (about 1.5 kg/3 lb)
¼ Spanish onion, finely chopped
8 button mushrooms, finely chopped
2–3 level tablespoons butter
2–3 level tablespoons finely chopped parsley
salt and freshly ground black pepper
150 ml/¼ pint double cream or dry white
   wine

1. Sauté finely chopped onion and mushrooms in
butter until onion is transparent.

2. Have fish cleaned and scaled. Wipe it well with
a damp cloth and place it in a well-buttered
shallow baking dish in which you have sprinkled
half the onion and mushroom mixture. Cover
fish with remaining onions and mushrooms and
season with finely chopped parsley, salt and
freshly ground black pepper to taste. Pour over
double cream or dry white wine. Bake in a
moderately hot oven (190°C, 375°F, Gas Mark 5)
until fish flakes easily with a fork. Serve immediately in the casserole.

Sautéed Salmon Steaks

4 fresh salmon steaks
2 tablespoons flour
4–6 level tablespoons butter
1 tablespoon olive oil
150 ml/¼ pint dry white wine
1 bay leaf
salt
white pepper
pinch of celery seed
2–4 level tablespoons finely chopped parsley

1. Choose centre cuts of salmon about 1.5 cm/¾
inch thick. Rub steaks well on both sides with flour.

2. Melt butter with olive oil in a heavy frying pan
or French casserole, and when hot sauté steaks
lightly. When steaks are light brown, add white
wine and seasonings. Cover and simmer on top of
stove until cooked, about 30 minutes, basting
frequently. When salmon is cooked, sprinkle with
finely chopped parsley and serve.

Salmon Brochettes

2–3 fresh salmon steaks (about 3.5 cm/1½
    inches thick)
6 tablespoons olive oil
2 tablespoons lemon juice
½ Spanish onion, finely chopped
4–6 level tablespoons finely chopped parsley
salt and freshly ground black pepper
4 small onions, sliced
4 tomatoes, sliced
16 small bay leaves
lemon juice

1. Cut fresh salmon steaks into bite-sized cubes and marinate for at least 2 hours in olive oil, lemon juice, finely chopped onion, parsley, salt and freshly ground black pepper, to taste.

2. Place fish cubes on a skewer alternating with a slice of onion, a slice of tomato and a bay leaf. Grill over charcoal or under the grill, turning frequently and basting from time to time with marinade sauce.

3. To serve: remove cooked fish from skewer on to serving plate and sprinkle with lemon juice.

Cold Salmon with Watercress Mousseline

Illustrated on page 28

4 fresh salmon steaks
600 ml/1 pint water
½ Spanish onion, sliced
1 stick celery, sliced
1 bay leaf
juice of 1 lemon
salt and freshly ground black pepper

WATERCRESS MOUSSELINE
2 bunches watercress
150 ml/¼ pint double cream
salt and freshly ground black pepper

1. Combine water, sliced onion, celery, bay leaf, lemon juice, salt and freshly ground black pepper to taste, in a wide saucepan. Bring to the boil, then reduce heat and simmer gently for 15 minutes.

2. Add salmon steaks to the simmering liquid, carefully placing them on the bottom of the saucepan without letting them overlap. Cover pan and simmer for 10 minutes, or until fish flakes easily with a fork.

3. Chill the steaks in their own liquid and drain just before serving. Serve with Watercress Mousseline.

4. To make Watercress Mousseline: remove leaves from watercress and place them in cold water. Bring to the boil and then simmer for 10 minutes. Rinse well in cold water, drain and pass through a fine sieve. Bring double cream to the boil in a saucepan, add sieved watercress and season to taste with salt and freshly ground black pepper. Chill. Just before serving, whisk until thick and smooth.

15

Sole en Papillote 'Festa del Mare' *Serves 4*
Baked English Trout with Bacon *Serves 4*
Stuffed Trout with White Wine *Serves 4 to 6*

16

Sole en Papillote 'Festa del Mare'

4 small sole, filleted
flour
salt and freshly ground black pepper
4 level tablespoons butter
2 tablespoons olive oil
4–6 button mushrooms, thinly sliced
4 tablespoons frozen prawns
4 tablespoons cockles
1 clove garlic, finely chopped
2 level tablespoons chopped parsley
150 ml/¼ pint dry white wine
150 ml/¼ pint double cream

1. Flour fillets and season to taste with salt and freshly ground black pepper. Sauté fillets gently on each side in butter and olive oil. Add sliced mushrooms, prawns, cockles, finely chopped garlic, parsley and dry white wine. Bring to the boil and reduce wine to half the original quantity. Add cream, lower heat and simmer gently for about 10 minutes, or until fish flakes with a fork.

2. To make papillotes: cut 4 pieces of paper (or foil) in pieces approximately 21 cm by 28 cm/8½ by 11 inches. Fold in half and cut into heart shapes. Open paper (or foil), brush with oil and place 4 fish fillets on each piece. Garnish with mushroom mixture and pour over sauce. Fold paper or foil shapes over and seal edges well by crimping them firmly together.

3. Place *papillotes* in an ovenproof dish, pour over a little olive oil and bake in a moderately hot oven (200°C, 400°F, Gas Mark 6) for 10 minutes. Arrange on a serving platter, slit edges of *papillotes*, roll back and serve immediately.

Baked English Trout with Bacon

4 fresh trout
8 rashers bacon, trimmed
salt and freshly ground black pepper
4 level tablespoons finely chopped parsley
4 tablespoons melted butter

1. Clean trout, split them open and remove backbones.

2. Cover the bottom of a flameproof *gratin* dish or shallow baking dish with bacon slices. Lay the split fish on the bacon cut sides down and sprinkle with salt, freshly ground black pepper and finely chopped parsley.

3. Dribble with melted butter and bake in a moderately hot oven (190°C, 375°F, Gas Mark 5) for 20 to 30 minutes, until fish flakes easily with a fork. Serve from baking dish.

Stuffed Trout with White Wine

4–6 fresh trout
225 g/8 oz cod or hake
4 large mushrooms, finely chopped
2 level tablespoons butter
2 tablespoons olive oil
1 egg white
salt and freshly ground black pepper
150–300 ml/¼–½ pint double cream
300 ml/½ pint fish stock or canned clam juice
300 ml/½ pint dry white wine
4 shallots, finely chopped

SAUCE
2 level tablespoons butter
2 level tablespoons flour
150 ml/¼ pint fish stock
300 ml/½ pint double cream
1 egg yolk
few drops of lemon juice
flour
butter

1. Slit trout carefully down the back, bone and empty them. Remove bones and skin from cod or hake.

2. Sauté finely chopped mushrooms in butter and olive oil.

3. Pound cod or hake to a smooth paste in a mortar, pass through a wire sieve and pound in mortar again with raw egg white. Season to taste with salt and freshly ground black pepper. Place mixture in a bowl over ice for 1 hour, gradually working in cream by mixing with a spatula from time to time. Add sautéed mushrooms to this mixture, and stuff fish.

4. Just before serving, poach stuffed trout in fish stock (or canned clam juice) and dry white wine with shallots, salt and freshly ground black pepper, to taste.

5. When trout are cooked, place on a heated serving dish and pour sauce over them.

6. **To make sauce:** reduce fish stock over a high heat to a quarter of the original quantity. Melt 1 level tablespoon butter in the top of a double saucepan, add flour and make a *roux*. Add fish stock and simmer until thickened. Stir in double cream and egg yolk. Whisk in a few drops of lemon juice and remaining butter. If sauce seems too thin, thicken with a *beurre manié*, made by mixing equal quantities of flour and butter to a smooth paste. Heat until sauce is smooth and thick, stirring constantly. Strain sauce over fish and serve immediately.

Turbot au Beurre Blanc

1 turbot (about 2.25 kg/5 lb), cleaned and
   prepared
well-flavoured Court-Bouillon (see page 83)

BEURRE BLANC
4 shallots, finely chopped
150 ml/¼ pint white wine vinegar
dry white wine
100-225 g/4-8 oz butter, diced
few drops of lemon juice
salt and freshly ground black pepper

1. Place a small whole turbot in a well-flavoured simmering *court-bouillon*. Bring gently to the boil, skim and lower heat until the liquid barely simmers. Poach for 25 to 35 minutes, until flesh flakes easily with a fork.

2. Remove fish from *court-bouillon*, drain and arrange on a hot serving dish. Serve immediately with *Beurre Blanc*.

3. **To make Beurre Blanc:** simmer chopped shallots in wine vinegar for 1 hour, adding a little dry white wine if it becomes too dry. Strain this reduced sauce into a small saucepan and whisk in diced butter over a high heat until sauce becomes thick and smooth. Do not let sauce separate, or all you will have is melted butter. Add a few drops of lemon juice and season to taste with salt and freshly ground black pepper.

Note: Few kitchens are equipped with a fish kettle or pan large enough to deal with a whole turbot, so ask your fishmonger to cut turbot into more manageable portions.

Turbot au Gratin

1 kg/2 lb poached turbot, flaked
225-350 g/8-12 oz well-flavoured Cream
   Sauce (see page 89)
butter
4-6 level tablespoons freshly grated
   Parmesan cheese

1. Bring well-flavoured Cream Sauce to the boil in the top of a double saucepan, add flaked turbot and heat through.

2. Pour turbot and sauce into a well-buttered, shallow flameproof dish. Sprinkle with grated cheese, dot with butter and glaze under a pre-heated grill until sauce is golden and bubbly. Serve immediately.

Beef

Grilled Hamburgers

1 kg/2 lb rump steak, minced
6 level tablespoons chopped beef marrow
6 level tablespoons finely chopped parsley
6 level tablespoons finely chopped onion
salt and freshly ground black pepper
4 level tablespoons melted butter

1. Combine minced beef, chopped beef marrow, parsley and onion; season to taste with salt and freshly ground black pepper.

2. Form mixture lightly into 4 large patties. Brush patties with melted butter and place under a grill for 4 to 5 minutes on each side.

Mixed Grill 'Skuets'

225 g/8 oz boned sirloin
225 g/8 oz boned shoulder of lamb
225 g/8 oz lamb's kidney
4 tablespoons olive oil
4 tablespoons lemon juice
1 large clove garlic, finely chopped
$\frac{1}{2}$ level teaspoon each dried thyme and sage
mushroom caps
small white onions, parboiled

1. Cut beef and lamb into 5-cm/2-inch cubes and cut kidney into thinner pieces.

2. Marinate meats in olive oil and lemon juice with finely chopped garlic and herbs for at least 1 hour.

3. Thread meats on skewers with mushroom caps and small parboiled onions. Grill, basting with the oil and lemon marinade, until cooked.

Burgundy Beef Kebabs

1.5 kg/3 lb steak
350 g/12 oz mushroom caps
2–3 green peppers, cut into 2.5-cm/1-inch squares

BURGUNDY MARINADE
150 ml/$\frac{1}{4}$ pint olive oil
6 tablespoons red Burgundy
2 tablespoons lemon juice
2 tablespoons soy sauce
1–2 cloves garlic, finely chopped
$\frac{1}{4}$ level teaspoon dry mustard
$\frac{1}{4}$ level teaspoon dried thyme
4 level tablespoons finely chopped celery
$\frac{1}{2}$ Spanish onion, coarsely chopped
salt and freshly ground black pepper

1. Cut meat into 2.5-cm/1-inch cubes.

2. Combine Burgundy Marinade ingredients in a large bowl. Add meat, stir well and refrigerate overnight. When ready to use, drain meat and reserve marinade.

3. When ready to grill: arrange beef cubes on long skewers, alternating with mushroom caps and green pepper squares. Grill over hot coals, turning meat and basting from time to time, until cooked as you like it.

California Beef Kebabs

1 kg/2 lb tender beef
4 tablespoons soy sauce
8 tablespoons olive oil
8 level tablespoons finely chopped onion
1-2 cloves garlic, crushed
freshly ground black pepper
¼ level teaspoon powdered cumin
green and red pepper squares
button onions, parboiled
tomatoes, quartered

1. Cut beef into 2.5-cm/1-inch cubes and marinate in soy sauce, olive oil, chopped onion, garlic, freshly ground black pepper and powdered cumin for at least 2 hours.

2. When ready to cook, arrange beef on skewers alternating with squares of green and red peppers, small white onions and quartered tomatoes. Grill over hot coals, turning meat and basting from time to time, until cooked as you like it.

Pork and Beef Kebabs

450 g/1 lb pork, cut from leg
450 g/1 lb round beef steak
225 g/8 oz Spanish onions, finely chopped
salt and freshly ground black pepper
olive oil
4-6 tomatoes, halved
4-6 small onions, poached
2 baby marrows, sliced
4-6 mushroom caps

1. Have pork and beef cut into steaks about 2.5 cm/1 inch thick and cut steaks into 5-cm/2-inch squares. Combine meats and finely chopped Spanish onions in a bowl with salt, freshly ground black pepper and 6 to 8 tablespoons olive oil. Toss well, cover bowl and refrigerate overnight.

2. When ready to cook: remove meat from onion mixture (reserving onions for later use). Arrange pork and beef on 4 to 6 skewers alternating with tomato halves, poached onions, slices of baby marrow and a mushroom cap.

3. Brush meat and vegetables lightly with olive oil and cook over charcoal or under cooker grill until done, turning skewers frequently and basting several times during cooking. Roll skewers in reserved onion mixture and serve immediately.

Grilled Steak with Roquefort Butter
Illustrated on page 68

1 large rump steak (about 3 cm/1¼ inches thick and weighing 675 g-1 kg/1½-2 lb)
freshly ground black pepper
butter
salt
25 g/2 oz Roquefort cheese
juice of ½ lemon
4 level tablespoons finely chopped parsley, chervil or chives

1. Remove steak from refrigerator at least 30 minutes before cooking. Slit fat around side to prevent meat from curling during cooking.

2. Preheat grill for 15 to 20 minutes.

3. Sprinkle both sides of steak with freshly ground black pepper and spread with 2 to 4 level tablespoons softened butter.

4. Rub hot grill with a piece of suet, place steak on grid and grill for 4 minutes on each side for a rare steak, 5 minutes on each side for medium, and for 6 to 8 minutes if you prefer steak to be well-done. Sprinkle with salt, to taste.

5. Cream Roquefort cheese and 50 g/2 oz butter with lemon juice and finely chopped parsley, chervil or chives. Season with salt and freshly ground black pepper, to taste.

6. Transfer steak to a heated serving platter and top with Roquefort butter.

19

20

Japanese Teriyaki 'Pan American'

675 g/1½ lb rump steak
2-4 tablespoons soy sauce
4 tablespoons sake or medium sherry
  diluted with water
4 tablespoons chicken stock
honey
freshly ground black pepper

1. Cut steak into 2.5-cm/1-inch cubes and marinate for at least 30 minutes in a mixture of soy sauce, *sake* (or medium sherry diluted with a little water), chicken stock and flavour to taste with honey.

2. Thread the beef on skewers and brush with marinade. Grill over charcoal or under the grill until meat is cooked to your liking, turning the skewers from time to time. Season with freshly ground black pepper, to taste.

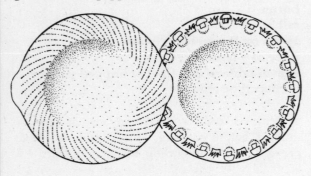

Grilled Steak 'Fines Herbes'

1 large rump steak (about 3 cm/1¼ inches
  thick and weighing 675 g-1 kg/1½-2 lb)
freshly ground black pepper
butter
salt
2 level tablespoons chopped chives
2 level tablespoons chopped parsley
¼ lemon
thin slices of beef marrow

1. Remove steak from refrigerator at least 30 minutes before cooking. Slit fat in several places around side to prevent meat from curling during cooking.

2. Preheat grill for 15 to 20 minutes.

3. Sprinkle both sides of steak with freshly ground black pepper and spread with 2 to 4 level tablespoons softened butter.

4. Rub hot grill with a piece of suet, place steak on grid and grill for 4 minutes on each side for a rare steak, 5 minutes on each side for medium, and for 6 to 8 minutes if you prefer steak to be well-done. Sprinkle with salt, to taste.

5. Make a sauce of 6 level tablespoons butter combined with chopped chives, parsley and pan juices. Season with lemon juice, salt and freshly ground black pepper, to taste.

6. Transfer steak to a heated serving platter and pour sauce over it. Top with slices of beef marrow poached for 4 minutes in salted water.

Beefsteak with Oyster Sauce

1 large thick rump steak (about 3 cm/1¼
  inches thick and weighing 675 g-1 kg/
  1½-2 lb)
freshly ground black pepper
softened butter

OYSTER SAUCE
12 oysters
2 level tablespoons butter
1-2 tablespoons lemon juice
salt
cayenne
2 egg yolks
6 level tablespoons double cream
Worcestershire sauce

1. Remove steak from refrigerator at least 30 minutes before cooking. Slit fat in several places around sides to prevent meat from curling during cooking.

2. Preheat grill for 15 minutes.

3. Sprinkle both sides of steak with freshly ground black pepper and spread with softened butter. Grill on each side for 4 minutes for a rare steak, 5 minutes for medium, and for 6 to 8 minutes to be well-done. In the meantime, make the sauce.

4. To make Oyster Sauce: remove oysters from shells, saving the liquor. Combine oysters and liquor in a saucepan with butter, lemon juice, salt and cayenne to taste. Simmer gently for 2 to 3 minutes until the oysters begin to curl up. Remove pan from heat and stir in egg yolks beaten with cream. Add a little Worcestershire sauce, to taste, and heat through, but do not allow to come to a boil again or sauce will curdle. Keep sauce warm over hot water.

5. To serve: place steak on hot serving dish and surround with Oyster Sauce.

Steak Poele 'Paul Chêne'

4 thick steaks
salt and freshly ground black pepper
4 level tablespoons butter
2 tablespoons hot beef stock
juice of $\frac{1}{2}$ lemon
2 level tablespoons finely chopped parsley
2 level tablespoons finely chopped chervil
    or chives

1. Season steaks generously with salt and freshly ground black pepper, and sauté on both sides in butter until cooked as you like them.

2. Place steaks on a heated dish. Add hot stock and lemon juice to pan juices and pour over the meat. Sprinkle with finely chopped herbs and serve immediately.

Pepper Steak

4 thick fillet steaks
salt
2 level tablespoons crushed peppercorns
4 level tablespoons butter
2 tablespoons olive oil
dash of cognac
8 tablespoons well-flavoured veal stock
4 level tablespoons double cream

1. Flatten steaks and season to taste with salt. Press crushed peppercorns well into each side of meat. Sauté steaks on each side in 2 tablespoons

butter and 1 tablespoon olive oil until tender. Remove and keep warm.

2. Add a dash of cognac to the pan, pour in veal stock and cook over a high heat, stirring occasionally, until stock is reduced to half of the original quantity. Add remaining butter and shake pan vigorously until butter is amalgamated into sauce. Add cream and continue to shake pan until sauce is rich and smooth.

3. Pour sauce over steaks and serve immediately.

Entrecôtes Bercy

2 sirloin steaks (about 450 g/1 lb each)
sprigs of fresh watercress

BERCY SAUCE
100g/4 oz beef marrow, diced
4 shallots, finely chopped
300 ml/$\frac{1}{2}$ pint dry white wine
225 g/8 oz softened butter, diced
4 level tablespoons finely chopped parsley
2 tablespoons lemon juice
salt and freshly ground black pepper

1. To make Bercy Sauce: poach diced beef marrow in boiling water, drain and cool. Simmer finely chopped shallots in white wine until the liquid is reduced to a third of the original quantity. Remove from heat and whisk until slightly cooled, then with pan over hot but not boiling water, gradually whisk in diced softened butter stirring continuously until sauce is thickened. Stir in diced beef marrow, finely chopped parsley, lemon juice, and season to taste with salt and freshly ground black pepper.

2. Grill steaks for 2 to 3 minutes on each side for rare, 4 minutes for medium and 5 to 6 minutes for well-done. Place on a heated serving dish and garnish with sprigs of fresh watercress. Serve immediately with Bercy Sauce.

21

22

Planked Steak

1 large rump steak (about 3 cm/1¼ inches
   thick and weighing 675 g–1 kg/1½–2 lb)
freshly ground black pepper
4 level tablespoons softened butter
salt
olive oil
Glazed Onions (see below)
Grilled Tomatoes (see below)
buttered peas
Pommes de Terre Duchesse (see page 23)
sprigs of watercress

1. Remove steak from refrigerator at least 30 minutes before cooking. Slit fat in several places around side to prevent meat from curling during cooking.

2. Preheat grill for 15 to 20 minutes.

3. Sprinkle both sides of steak with freshly ground black pepper and spread with softened butter.

4. Rub hot grill with a piece of suet and place steak on grid. Grill on each side for 4 minutes for a rare steak, 5 minutes for medium, and for 6 to 8 minutes to be well-done. Sprinkle with salt, to taste.

5. Place steak on a plank or wooden platter that has been oiled thoroughly with olive oil and heated in the oven. Arrange Glazed Onions, Grilled Tomatoes and buttered peas around steak, and garnish with a ring of Pommes de Terre Duchesse. Brown under grill and garnish with fresh watercress.

Glazed Onions

12 small onions
salt
1 tablespoon butter
1 tablespoon granulated sugar

1. Cook small white onions in boiling salted water until they are tender and drain well.

2. Melt butter in a saucepan, add sugar and stir until well blended. Add onions and cook slowly until they are glazed. Keep warm.

Grilled Tomatoes

6 large ripe tomatoes
butter
salt and freshly ground black pepper
dried oregano
1–2 tablespoons breadcrumbs
1 teaspoon finely chopped chives or onion
1–2 tablespoons freshly grated Parmesan
   cheese

1. Cut tomatoes in half.

2. Place tomato halves in a buttered baking dish. Season to taste with salt, freshly ground black pepper and dried oregano. Sprinkle with breadcrumbs, finely chopped chives or onion, and freshly grated Parmesan. Dot tomatoes with butter and grill them 7.5 cm/3 inches from the heat until tender.

Pommes de Terre Duchesse

1 kg/2 lb potatoes
salt
2-4 level tablespoons butter
2 eggs
2 egg yolks
freshly ground black pepper
freshly grated nutmeg

1. Peel potatoes and slice them thickly. Cover and cook them in simmering salted water until soft but not mushy. Drain well and return potatoes to pan and remove all moisture by shaking pan over heat until they are dry.

2. Rub potatoes through a fine sieve and add butter, beating with a wooden spoon until mixture is very smooth.

3. Combine eggs and egg yolks, and gradually beat into potato mixture. Season to taste with salt, freshly ground black pepper and freshly grated nutmeg. Beat until mixture is very fluffy.

Tournedos en Croûte

4 tournedos
4 level tablespoons butter
2 tablespoons olive oil
4 mushrooms finely chopped
100 g/4 oz pâté de foie gras, crumbled
salt and freshly ground black pepper
2-4 tablespoons dry sherry or Madeira
Flaky Pastry (see page 91)
1 egg, separated

1. Sauté *tournedos* in 2 level tablespoons butter and olive oil for about 3 minutes on each side. Remove from pan and allow to cool.

2. Sauté mushrooms in the remaining butter until golden. Add crumbled *pâté de foie gras* and sauté the mixture until lightly browned. Season to taste with salt and freshly ground black pepper, and enough sherry or Madeira to bind the mixture. Spread the top of each *tournedos* thinly with this mixture and allow to cool.

3. Cut 4 rounds of flaky pastry 2.5 cm/1 inch larger in diameter than the meat, and the same number about 3.5 cm/1½ inches larger in diameter.

4. Lay *tournedos* on the smaller rounds and cover them with the larger ones. Brush pastry edges with lightly beaten egg white and press together firmly. Decorate pastry tops with cut out leaves, etc. and paint with lightly beaten egg yolk.

5. Bake in a moderately hot oven (200°C, 400°F, Gas Mark 6) for 15 to 20 minutes, or until the pastry is golden.

Note: For a more inexpensive version of this dish, substitute the *foie gras* with ½ Spanish onion and 2 thin slices of cooked ham, both finely chopped and sautéed in butter until golden.

Tournedos 'En Boite'

4 thickly cut tournedos
4 level tablespoons butter
6 finely chopped shallots
French mustard
Worcestershire sauce
pinch of rosemary
salt and freshly ground black pepper
4 tablespoons cognac

1. Place well-trimmed *tournedos* in 4 individual flameproof casseroles with butter and finely chopped shallots, flavoured to taste with French mustard and Worcestershire sauce.

2. Cover and cook for about 5 minutes then drain fat, turn *tournedos* over and add a pinch each of rosemary, salt and freshly ground black pepper to each casserole. Pour cognac over meat, cover and continue cooking for a few minutes longer. Serve in casseroles.

23

Steak in Beer *Serves 4*
Texas Beef with Oysters *Serves 4 to 6*
Mr Pickwick's Boiled Dinner *Serves 8 to 10*

Steak in Beer

24

1 thick rump steak (1 kg/2 lb)
4 tablespoons olive oil
1 clove garlic, finely chopped
salt and freshly ground black pepper
450 g/1 lb button mushrooms, sliced
4–6 level tablespoons butter
juice of ¼ lemon
2 level tablespoons flour
300 ml/½ pint beer
1–2 teaspoons soy sauce

1. Brush steak with olive oil, sprinkle with ½ clove finely chopped garlic and season to taste with salt and freshly ground black pepper. Allow steak to absorb these flavours for at least 1 hour. Grill until medium rare.

2. A few minutes before the steak is done, sauté sliced mushrooms in butter and lemon juice until tender. Add flour and stir until well blended then pour in beer. Bring the mixture to the boil. Add soy sauce and remaining finely chopped garlic and season to taste with freshly ground black pepper.

3. Place steak on a heated serving dish and pour bubbling mushroom and beer sauce over meat. Serve immediately.

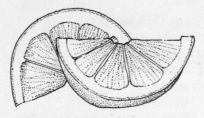

Texas Beef with Oysters
Illustrated on page 65

1.5 kg/3 lb sirloin joint
4 tablespoons softened butter
freshly ground black pepper
salt
1 dozen fresh oysters, drained
2 tablespoons finely chopped parsley
lemon wedges

1. Rub joint with softened butter and freshly ground black pepper, to taste. Roast in a hot oven

(220°C, 425°F, Gas Mark 7) for 15 minutes. Reduce the heat to moderately hot (190°C, 375°F, Gas Mark 5) and continue to roast for 1 hour.

2. Remove joint from the oven. Season to taste with salt, and place the drained fresh oysters over the meat. Cook for a further 5 to 10 minutes, or until the oysters plump up and begin to crinkle at the edges. Sprinkle with finely chopped parsley, and serve with lemon wedges.

Mr Pickwick's Boiled Dinner

1.75 kg/4 lb shoulder of beef
450 g/1 lb salt pork
2 bay leaves
6 peppercorns
1 boiling chicken, drawn
1 loin of pork
8 large carrots, scraped
8 medium onions, peeled
8 large potatoes, peeled
8 small turnips, peeled and quartered

HORSERADISH CHANTILLY
whipped cream
salt
freshly grated horseradish

1. Ask your butcher to bone and tie beef. Place in a large stockpot or heavy-bottomed saucepan with just enough cold water to cover and bring to the boil. Skim and reduce heat to a simmer. Add salt pork, bay leaves and peppercorns, cover and simmer over the lowest of heats for 3 to 4 hours, skimming from time to time, until meat is tender. Add chicken and fresh pork after first hour.

2. Cool slightly and skim off any excess fat. Add carrots, onions, potatoes and turnips and cook for 20 to 30 minutes, until vegetables are tender.

3. Serve the beef, pork, salt pork and chicken on a platter garnished with vegetables. Accompany with Horseradish Chantilly.

4. To make Horseradish Chantilly: stir salt into whipped cream and add freshly grated horse-radish to taste.

Grilled Sea Bass aux Herbes (see page 12)

Roast Leg of Pork Cooked Like Game (see page 56)

Spiedini di Vitello alla Romana (see page 42)

Roast Loin of Pork (see page 53)

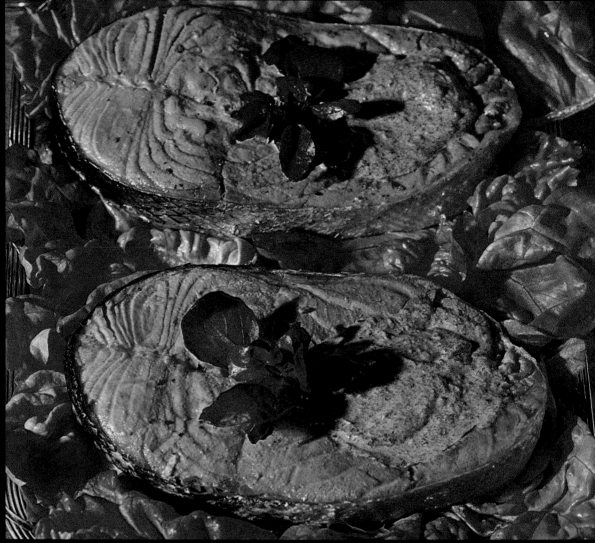

Cold Salmon with Watercress Mousseline (see page 15)

Fish Souvlakia (see page 13)

Rare Fillet Stroganoff 'Four Seasons'
Illustrated on page 68

8-12 slices fillet of beef
4 tablespoons melted butter
paprika
rich beef stock or jus de viande
1-2 tablespoons brandy
1 tablespoon dry sherry
125 ml/¼ pint soured cream
lemon juice
salt and freshly ground black pepper

1. Sauté beef in melted butter for a minute or two on each side. Sprinkle with paprika, add rich beef stock or *jus de viande*. Cover and simmer gently until meat is done to your liking.

2. Remove meat and keep warm. Add brandy and sherry to juices and reduce sauce to the desired consistency. Add soured cream, being careful not to bring sauce to the boil after soured cream is added. Sprinkle lemon juice to taste into sauce, add salt and freshly ground black pepper if necessary.

Barbecued Beef in Foil

1 kg/2 lb round of beef
olive oil
4 medium-sized onions, quartered
4 medium-sized carrots

TOMATO BARBECUE SAUCE
½ small onion
1 clove garlic
1 sprig parsley
150 ml/¼ pint tomato ketchup
2 tablespoons wine vinegar
2 tablespoons olive oil
1 teaspoon Worcestershire sauce
freshly ground black pepper

1. To make Tomato Barbecue Sauce: finely chop onion, garlic and parsley and put in a large screw-top jar with all the other ingredients. Cover and shake vigorously until all ingredients are well blended. Allow to stand for 24 hours before using.

2. Brush round of beef on both sides with oil and grill until well browned on both sides.

3. Place it on a double sheet of foil large enough to fold over roast. Add quartered onions and carrots, and coat with Tomato Barbecue Sauce. Fold foil over roast and cook for 45 to 60 minutes, until meat is tender.

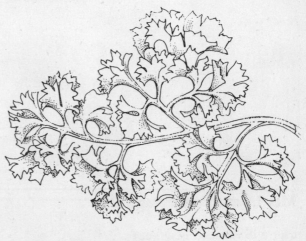

Beef and Pork Loaf

1 kg/2 lb each lean beef and pork
1 Spanish onion, quartered
100 g/4 oz fresh breadcrumbs
milk
1 (227-g/8-oz) can Italian tomatoes
3 eggs, well beaten
2 bay leaves, crumbled
salt and freshly ground black pepper
thyme
6-8 tablespoons heated stock
French Tomato Sauce (see page 90)

1. Put beef, pork and quartered onion through mincer twice and mix well with fresh bread-crumbs which you have moistened with a little milk. Then add canned tomatoes, well-beaten eggs, crumbled bay leaves, salt, freshly ground black pepper and thyme, to taste. Mix well.

2. Put mixture in a well-greased baking dish, or pat into a loaf shape on a greased baking sheet or oiled board. Bake in a moderate oven (160°C, 325°F, Gas Mark 3) for at least 1 hour, basting occasionally with a little hot stock. Serve with French Tomato Sauce.

30

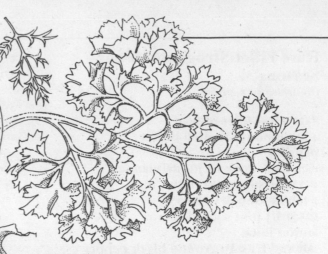

Mrs Beeton's Cottage Pie

1 kg/2 lb minced raw beef
1½ Spanish onions, chopped
butter
6 medium-sized carrots, minced
2 level tablespoons tomato purée
2–4 level tablespoons finely chopped herbs
   (parsley, thyme, bay leaf, chervil, or
   sage, etc.)
beef stock
salt and freshly ground black pepper
450 g/1 lb potatoes, cooked

1. Sauté chopped onions in butter until transparent then add minced beef and sauté stirring continuously, until brown.

2. Stir in minced carrot, tomato purée and finely chopped herbs. Add sufficient beef stock to cover and season to taste with salt and freshly ground black pepper. Simmer for 30 to 40 minutes, until meat is tender. Place meat mixture in a well-buttered deep oval pie dish.

3. Mash cooked potatoes and season to taste with clarified butter, salt and freshly ground black pepper. Pile mixture on meat and brown in a moderately hot oven (200°C, 400°F, Gas Mark 6) for 8 to 10 minutes, until golden.

Fresh or Salt Brisket with Horseradish Sauce

1.5–1.75 kg/3–4 lb fresh or salt beef brisket
2 Spanish onions, each stuck with a clove
4 large carrots
2 bay leaves
salt and freshly ground black pepper

HORSERADISH SAUCE
2 level tablespoons butter
2 level tablespoons flour
300 ml/¼ pint hot milk
150 ml/¼ pint reduced stock from brisket
4–6 level tablespoons grated horseradish
1 tablespoon lemon juice
salt and freshly ground black pepper

1. Place meat in a casserole with onions, carrots and bay leaves, and cover with water. Season with salt (no salt if salt beef is used) and freshly ground black pepper and bring gently to the boil. Skim; lower heat and simmer very gently for 3 to 4 hours, until meat is tender. Cool in stock.

2. Slice meat thinly and reheat in stock just before serving. Serve with Horseradish Sauce.

3. To make Horseradish Sauce: melt butter in the top of a double saucepan, add flour and cook for 1 minute, stirring constantly, until smooth. Add hot milk and reduced stock from brisket (reduce 300 ml/½ pint stock to half of its original quantity) stirring continuously until mixture comes to the boil. Drain horseradish, add it to sauce with lemon juice, and season to taste with salt and freshly ground black pepper.

Old English Beefsteak and Kidney Pie *Serves 4 to 6*
Steamed Beef – Chinese Style *Serves 2 to 4*
Island Paper-wrapped Beef *Serves 2 to 3*

Old English Beefsteak and Kidney Pie

Illustrated on page 68

1 kg/2 lb thick beefsteak, cut into 3.5-cm/
 1½-inch cubes
350 g/12 oz calf's kidney
4 level tablespoons plain flour
1 level tablespoon salt
¾ level teaspoon freshly ground black
 pepper
6 level tablespoons butter or suet
1 Spanish onion, finely chopped
300 ml/½ pint rich beef stock
1 bay leaf
1 level tablespoon chopped parsley
¼ level teaspoon each powdered cloves and
 marjoram
Flaky Pastry (see page 91)

1. Clean kidney, split in half, remove fat and large tubes, and soak in salted water for 1 hour. Dry kidney and cut into 5-mm/¼-inch slices.

2. Mix flour, salt and ½ level teaspoon freshly ground black pepper, and roll beef and kidneys in this mixture.

3. Melt butter or suet in a thick-bottomed casserole and sauté finely chopped onion until golden. Add the beef and kidneys, and brown them thoroughly, stirring almost constantly. Moisten with beef stock and add remaining freshly ground black pepper, bay leaf, chopped parsley, powdered cloves and marjoram. Mix well, cover casserole and simmer over a low flame for 1 to 1¼ hours, until meat is tender. If liquid is too thin, thicken with a little flour mixed to a paste with water.

4. Butter a deep baking dish, place a pie funnel in centre of dish, add meats and liquid and allow to cool.

5. In the meantime, make flaky pastry and place over meat, moistening and pinching edges to dish. Make vents in the pastry to allow steam to escape and bake in a hot oven (230°C, 450°F, Gas Mark 8) for 10 minutes. Lower heat to moderately hot (190°C, 375°F, Gas Mark 5) and continue baking for 15 minutes, or until pastry crust is golden.

Steamed Beef – Chinese Style

31

450 g/1 lb beefsteak
1 teaspoon cornflour
salt and freshly ground black pepper
2 teaspoons soy sauce
1 tablespoon oil
2 tablespoons sherry
1 teaspoon wine vinegar
2 spring onions

1. Slice beefsteak across the grain into thin strips and place in a bowl.

2. Blend cornflour, salt, freshly ground black pepper, soy sauce, oil, sherry and vinegar, and pour over beef. Chop the onions very finely and sprinkle over top. Cover tightly and let stand for at least 1 hour.

3. When ready to cook: place bowl of beef on a stand over a saucepan of boiling water. Cover saucepan and steam until beef is tender. Serve immediately.

Island Paper-wrapped Beef

350 g/12 oz tender beefsteak
3 tablespoons sake or dry sherry
3 tablespoons soy sauce
1 level tablespoon cornflour
1 Spanish onion, finely chopped
oiled paper
peanut oil for frying

1. Slice beef thinly across the grain and marinate in *sake* (or dry sherry), soy sauce, cornflour and finely chopped onion for 10 to 15 minutes, stirring from time to time.

2. Divide the beef into equal portions on 10-cm/ 4-inch squares of oiled paper (18 to 20 squares) and fold securely into little packets.

3. Deep-fry the packages in hot oil for 2 minutes and serve hot, just as they are in their little paper jackets.

Serves 4 to 5 as an appetiser, if one or two other dishes are served.

Chinese Steak with Green Peppers *Serves 2 to 4*
Roast Prime Ribs of Beef *Serves 8 to 10*
Roast Fillet of Beef *Serves 8 to 12*

32

Chinese Steak with Green Peppers

450 g/1 lb rump steak
4 tablespoons corn or peanut oil
1 small clove garlic
¼ Spanish onion, diced
1 green pepper, diced
salt and freshly ground black pepper
¼ teaspoon ginger
1 level tablespoon cornflour
150 ml/¼ pint well-flavoured stock
1-2 teaspoons soy sauce

1. Cut steak diagonally across the grain into thin slices, then cut into strips about 5 cm/2 inches long.

2. Heat oil in frying pan over medium heat. Place garlic clove in hot oil and remove after 3 minutes. Add meat to oil and stir-fry over medium heat until meat starts to brown. Mix in onion, green pepper, salt, freshly ground black pepper and ginger, and cook over medium heat, stirring constantly until tender – about 3 minutes.

3. Blend cornflour with stock and soy sauce. Stir mixture into frying pan, bring to the boil and cook, stirring constantly, until liquid is thickened. Serve over rice.

Roast Prime Ribs of Beef
Illustrated on page 67

1 rib roast of beef (2.25–3.5 kg/5–8 lb)
2 cloves garlic, cut in slivers
2 bay leaves, crumbled
4–6 level tablespoons butter or fat
freshly ground black pepper
1 flattened piece of beef suet, to cover roast
4–6 tablespoons red wine or water
salt

1. Make 8 incisions in rib roast near the bone with the point of a sharp knife. Insert a sliver of garlic and a segment of bay leaf into each incision.

2. Spread beef with butter or fat and sprinkle with freshly ground black pepper. Tie a flattened layer of beef suet over the top and allow meat to absorb flavours for 2 hours before roasting.

3. Preheat oven to hot (220°C, 425°F, Gas Mark 8).

4. When ready to roast, place the meat on a rack over a roasting tin, resting meat on the bone ends, and roast for 15 minutes, then reduce oven to moderate (160°C, 325°F, Gas Mark 3). Add warmed red wine or water to pan and continue to roast, basting frequently, allowing 15 to 18 minutes per half kilo/per lb if you like your beef rare, 20 to 25 minutes per half kilo/per lb for medium, and 28 to 32 minutes per half kilo/per lb if you prefer it well-done.

5. When meat is cooked to your liking, season to taste with salt and additional pepper, remove to a warm serving platter and let it stand for 15 to 20 minutes at the edge of the open oven before carving. During this time the beef sets, the cooking subsides and the roast is ready for carving.

6. In the meantime, spoon off the excess fat in the roasting tin and using the pink juices that pour from the roast as it sets, stir all the crusty bits into it to make a clear sauce. Bring to the boil, reduce heat and simmer for 1 or 2 minutes. Strain and serve in a sauceboat with roast.

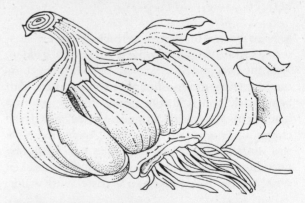

Roast Fillet of Beef

1 fillet of beef (1.75–2.75 kg/4–6 lb), stripped of fat
olive oil or melted butter
freshly ground black pepper
salt
mushrooms, sautéed in butter
baked potatoes

Fillet of beef, the most tender of all beef cuts,

cooks in a short time. At its best when served crusty brown outside and pink to rare inside, it should be roasted in a hot oven.

1. To roast fillet: place fillet on rack in a shallow roasting tin, tucking narrow end of fillet under to make the roast evenly thick. Brush generously with olive oil or melted butter and season with freshly ground black pepper. Roast in a hot oven (230°C, 450°F, Gas Mark 8) for 45 to 60 minutes, until beef is cooked to your liking.

2. Slice in 2.5-cm/1-inch slices, season with salt, and serve with sautéed mushrooms and baked potatoes.

Braised Beef in Pastry

1 boned loin of beef (about 1.5 kg/3 lb)
100 g/4 oz butter
2 tablespoons olive oil
100 g/4 oz unsmoked bacon, diced
300 ml/½ pint dry white wine
300 ml/½ pint well-flavoured beef stock
1 beef bone, sawn in pieces
1 calf's foot; split
salt and freshly ground black pepper
1 Spanish onion, finely chopped
450 g/1 lb button mushrooms, finely chopped
300 ml/½ pint well-flavoured Béchamel Sauce (see page 90)
Puff Pastry (see page 91)
1 egg, beaten

1. Melt half the butter in a thick-bottomed ovenproof casserole. Add olive oil and diced bacon, and sauté meat in this amalgamation of fats until well browned on all sides. Add dry white wine, stock, beef bone, calf's foot and barely enough hot water to cover the meat. Season to taste with salt and freshly ground black pepper. Cover casserole and simmer gently for 3½ to 4 hours.

2. Remove the meat from the liquid, raise heat and

boil the stock with bones and calf's foot until the sauce is reduced to a third of the original quantity.

3. Sauté finely chopped onion and mushrooms in remaining butter until onion is transparent. Add vegetable mixture to well-flavoured Béchamel Sauce and allow to cool.

4. Cut beef into slices and spread each slice thickly with Béchamel Sauce. Re-form the spread slices into a roast, slip a metal skewer as a marker between each slice. Divide the pastry in half, roll out each piece thinly and place roast on one half of pastry. Cover with remaining pastry, allowing handles of skewers to pierce through pastry, and seal edges well with beaten egg. Decorate with pastry leaves. Bake in a moderately hot oven (200°C, 400°F, Gas Mark 6) for about 40 minutes, or until pastry is cooked through and golden brown.

5. Strain sauce and serve with roast.

6. To carve roast: remove metal skewer markers from roast one by one, and slice pastry through where skewer was. In this way each piece of pre-sliced meat will have its own pastry case.

Roast Beef 'Redbridge'

4 thick slices rare roast beef
2 level tablespoons butter
1 tablespoon olive oil
meat juices left over from roast, skimmed of fat
1-2 level tablespoons Dijon mustard
4-6 tablespoons red wine
freshly ground black pepper
finely chopped chives

1. Melt butter and oil in a large frying pan and sauté beef slices until warmed through.

2. In the meantime, whisk meat juices with mustard until well blended. Pour over meat and allow to sizzle for a moment, then pour in red wine and turn up heat to reduce sauce. Season to taste with a little freshly ground black pepper and finely chopped chives.

33

Lamb

34

Brochettes de Mouton

1 kg/2 lb tender lamb
300 ml/½ pint olive oil
6 tablespoons lemon juice
1-2 level tablespoons honey
1 clove garlic, crushed
2 bay leaves, crushed
salt and freshly ground black pepper
green and red pepper squares
button onions, parboiled
tomatoes, quartered

1. Cut lamb into 2.5-cm/1-inch cubes.

2. Combine olive oil with lemon juice, honey, crushed garlic and bay leaves. Season to taste with salt and freshly ground black pepper, and marinate lamb in this mixture for 2 to 4 hours.

3. Thread cubes of meat on skewers alternately with squares of green and red peppers, button onions and quartered tomatoes, and grill for 15 to 20 minutes, brushing frequently with the marinade.

Lamb Steaks with Béarnaise Sauce

3 tender lamb steaks, cut from leg of
  baby lamb
salt and freshly ground black pepper
3-6 level tablespoons butter or lard
watercress
Béarnaise Sauce (see page 89)

1. Ask your butcher to cut 3 tender lamb steaks about 2.5 cm/1 inch thick from the large end of a leg of lamb. Bone the remainder and cut into 2.5-cm/1-inch cubes, and use for a curried lamb dish with rice.

2. Flatten lamb steaks with a cleaver and season with salt and freshly ground black pepper.

3. Melt butter or lard in a thick-bottomed frying pan. Place lamb steaks in pan and sauté in the hot fat for 6 minutes per side. Transfer to a heated serving dish and garnish with sprigs of fresh watercress. Serve immediately with Béarnaise Sauce.

Herb-breaded Lamb Cutlets

4-6 lamb cutlets or chops
100-175 g/4-6 oz dried breadcrumbs
2 level tablespoons finely chopped parsley
¼ level teaspoon dried thyme
¼ level teaspoon dried marjoram
grated rind of ½ lemon
salt and freshly ground black pepper
2 eggs, well beaten
4 tablespoons olive oil

1. Combine breadcrumbs, finely chopped parsley, dried thyme, marjoram and freshly grated lemon rind. Mix well.

2. Season lamb cutlets generously with salt and freshly ground black pepper. Dip in well-beaten egg and then coat with breadcrumb mixture.

3. Heat olive oil in a frying pan and sauté lamb cutlets over a low heat until they are well browned on both sides

Lamb Chops en Croûte 'Rainbow Room'

8 lamb chops, 3.5 cm/1½ inches thick
salt and freshly ground black pepper
olive oil
275 g/10 oz Puff Pastry (see page 91)
1 egg, beaten

DUXELLES
2 level tablespoons finely chopped shallots,
  or onion
4 level tablespoons butter
1 tablespoon olive oil
275 g/10 oz mushrooms, finely chopped
2 tablespoons Demi-glace or Brown Sauce
  (see page 83)
2 tablespoons finely chopped parsley
breadcrumbs, optional

1. Trim all fat from lamb chops and season with salt and freshly ground black pepper. Brown on both sides in a hot pan with a little olive oil. Chops should remain very rare on the inside. Cool.

2. To make duxelles: sauté chopped shallots, or onion, in butter and oil until transparent. Add chopped mushrooms (stalks and peels will do) and stir over a medium heat until moisture has evaporated. Add Demi-glace or Brown Sauce and finely chopped parsley. Let simmer for 5 minutes. Breadcrumbs may be added to achieve desired consistency.

3. Roll out puff pastry into 8 circles big enough to encase chops. Spread *duxelles* of mushrooms on top of chops. Place 1 chop on each circle of pastry and wrap around, leaving bone out. Moisten join with water and seal securely. Brush with beaten egg and bake in a moderately hot oven (200°C, 400°F, Gas Mark 6) for 15 minutes.

Grilled Lamb Cutlets 'Reforme'

8 small lamb cutlets
freshly ground black pepper
softened butter
salt

SAUCE
1–2 tablespoons vinegar
2 level tablespoons sugar
25 g/1 oz crushed peppercorns
1 onion, finely chopped
300 ml/½ pint well-flavoured Brown Sauce
   (see page 83)
100 g/4 oz tongue, cut en julienne
1 small beetroot, cut en julienne
white of 1 hard-boiled egg, cut en julienne
2 gherkins, cut en julienne

1. Remove lamb cutlets from refrigerator at least 30 minutes before cooking and trim fat.

2. Preheat grill.

3. Sprinkle both sides of cutlets with freshly ground black pepper, and spread with softened butter. Grill over charcoal or under grill until cooked. Sprinkle with salt and serve immediately

4. To make sauce: place vinegar, sugar, crushed peppercorns and finely chopped onion in a saucepan, and reduce over a high heat until onion is soft and highly flavoured. Add Brown Sauce and simmer for a few minutes. Strain and add slivers of tongue, beetroot, white of hard-boiled egg and gherkins.

Grilled Lamb Chops

Illustrated on page 48

8–10 tenderloin lamb chops
suet
lemon juice
rosemary or oregano
salt and freshly ground black pepper

1. Ask your butcher to trim a loin of baby lamb into 8 or 10 chops.

2. Preheat grill for 15 to 20 minutes. Rub grid with a piece of suet.

3. Place chops on grid, sprinkle with lemon juice and season to taste with rosemary or oregano, salt and freshly ground black pepper. Grill for 3 to 5 minutes on each side. Serve immediately.

Carré d'Agneau Persillé *Serves 4 to 6*
Lamb and Bacon Kebabs *Serves 6*
Leg of Lamb in Pastry 'L'Oustau de la Baumanière'*Serves 6*

36

Carré d'Agneau Persillé

Illustrated on page 45

2 loins of baby lamb
softened butter
salt and freshly ground black pepper
100 g/4 oz fresh breadcrumbs
4 tablespoons finely chopped parsley
½ level teaspoon dried thyme
½ level teaspoon dried marjoram
grated rind of ½ lemon
grilled whole tomatoes
watercress

1. Spread loins of lamb with softened butter and season generously with salt and freshly ground black pepper. Place in a roasting tin and roast in a moderately hot oven (200°C, 400°F, Gas Mark 6) for 15 minutes. Remove from oven and cool.

2. Make a paste of breadcrumbs, chopped parsley, thyme, marjoram, lemon rind and softened butter, and coat sides of lamb thickly with this mixture.

3. Twenty minutes before serving, return loins of lamb to a moderately hot oven and roast for 20 minutes.

4. Serve garnished with grilled whole tomatoes and watercress.

Lamb and Bacon Kebabs

Illustrated on page 48

675 g-1 kg/1½-2 lb boneless leg of lamb
4 tablespoons clear honey
2 tablespoons olive oil
2 tablespoons lemon juice
4 cloves garlic, crushed
2 tablespoons soy sauce
16 button onions, peeled
about 450 g/1 lb streaky bacon
2 large green peppers
8 black olives, stoned
2 large tomatoes, quartered

1. Cut lamb into 2.5-cm/1-inch cubes, discarding fat and gristle. You should have about 40 cubes. Put them in a bowl.

2. Combine next 5 ingredients with 300 ml/½ pint hot (not boiling) water. Pour over lamb and marinate for at least 1 hour.

3. Blanch button onions for 1 minute; drain well.

4. Stretch each bacon rasher out thinly with the back of a knife, and cut into pieces long enough to wrap around lamb cubes.

5. Halve, seed and core peppers. Cut each half into 3 strips and each strip in half (24 pieces).

6. Remove lamb from marinade and wrap each cube in a strip of bacon.

7. **Assemble eight 25-cm/10-inch skewers as follows:** 1 piece of pepper, 1 cube of lamb, 1 button onion, lamb, pepper, lamb, onion, lamb, pepper, lamb, black olive.

8. Barbecue skewers over hot coals, or under grill, turning occasionally and brushing with marinade. They will take 15 to 20 minutes.

9. Two or three minutes before the end of cooking time, spear a piece of tomato on to each skewer.

Leg of Lamb in Pastry 'L'Oustau de la Baumanière'

1 small leg of lamb, or piece of leg near
   bone (1.5 kg/3 lb)
2 lamb's kidneys, diced
butter
65 g/2½ oz mushrooms, sliced
1-2 truffles, diced (optional)
thyme and rosemary
salt and freshly ground black pepper
1-2 tablespoons Armagnac or good brandy
Flaky Pastry (see page 91)
1 egg yolk, slightly beaten

1. Ask your butcher to bone lamb, leaving shank end bone intact, so that you can stuff lamb. **Note:** if young lamb is not available, ask butcher to cut off 1-kg/3-lb piece near shank end, reserving top end of leg for lamb steaks or to cut into cubes for brochettes. Ask him to leave shank and bone intact.

2. Sauté kidneys in 2 tablespoons butter in a thick-bottomed frying pan for 1 minute. Add sliced mushrooms and diced truffles, and season to taste with thyme, rosemary, salt and freshly ground black pepper. Simmer, stirring constantly, for 1 or 2 minutes more. Sprinkle with Armagnac, or a good brandy.

3. Stuff leg of lamb with this mixture, reshape and stitch or tie opening with heavy thread. Sprinkle lamb with salt and freshly ground black pepper, and roast in a moderately hot oven (190°C, 375°F, Gas Mark 5) for 25 to 35 minutes, until half cooked.

4. Cool, rub with 2 tablespoons softened butter and wrap in thinly rolled Flaky Pastry. Brush with cold water and bake in a hot oven (230°C, 450°F, Gas Mark 8) for 20 minutes more. Brush with slightly beaten egg yolk and continue baking until the crust is browned and pastry is cooked.

Breaded Lamb Fingers Saint Germain

1–1.25 kg/2–2½ lb breast of lamb
1 Spanish onion, quartered
4 large carrots, quartered
450 ml/¾ pint well-flavoured veal or chicken stock
salt and freshly ground black pepper
flour
2 eggs, well beaten
breadcrumbs
4–6 tablespoons clarified butter
purée of green peas
Béarnaise Sauce (see page 89)

1. Poach lamb with Spanish onion and carrots in well-flavoured veal or chicken stock until tender, 1½ to 2 hours.

2. Carefully pull out the bones and place the meat on a flat dish, top with another dish and weight it lightly.

3. When cold, cut meat into thin strips about 3.5 cm/1½ inches wide. Trim strips neatly, season to taste with salt and freshly ground black pepper.

Roll strips in flour, dip in beaten egg and then roll in breadcrumbs.

4. Heat clarified butter in a thick-bottomed frying pan and sauté strips until golden brown. Arrange strips in a ring round a purée of green peas. Serve with Béarnaise Sauce.

Crown Roast of Lamb
Illustrated on page 47

1 crown roast of lamb, 16-rib (made from rib sections of two loins of lamb)
2 cloves garlic, slivered
1–2 level teaspoons rosemary
juice of 1 lemon
salt and freshly ground black pepper
softened butter
paper frills, or button mushroom caps simmered in butter
creamed button onions or buttered peas, or glazed button onions and mushrooms
finely chopped mint

1. Cut small slits in the lamb and insert slivers of garlic. Rub meat with rosemary and lemon juice, and sprinkle generously with salt and freshly ground black pepper. Brush with softened butter.

2. Cover tips of the crown's bones with foil to prevent them from burning as the roast cooks. Place the meat on a rack in an open roasting tin.

3. Cook crown of lamb in a cool oven (150°C, 300°F, Gas Mark 2) for about 2 to 2½ hours – it should be rare when served. Remove foil and replace with paper frills or mushroom caps simmered in butter. Fill the centre of the crown with creamed button onions or buttered peas, or a combination of glazed button onions and mushrooms; sprinkle with finely chopped mint and serve immediately.

37

Bourbon Barbecued Lamb *Serves 6*
Selle d'Agneau au Romarin *Serves 4 to 6*
Rack of Lamb with Harem Pilaff 'Rainbow Room'
Serves 4 to 6

38

Bourbon Barbecued Lamb

1 small leg of lamb, boned but not tied

MARINADE
150 ml/¼ pint bourbon whisky
150 ml/¼ pint olive oil
2 cloves garlic, finely chopped
2 bay leaves, crumbled
¼ level teaspoon each dried thyme, tarragon and rosemary
salt and freshly ground black pepper

1. Marinate lamb for 12 hours in marinade ingredients, turning meat several times during this period.

2. When ready to grill, build charcoal fire and burn until flames have subsided and coals are covered with ash. Drain lamb, reserving marinade. Place it on grill about 18 cm/7 inches from coals, and barbecue for 45 to 50 minutes, turning meat and brushing it with marinade every 10 minutes.

3. To serve: slice in thin strips and serve with rice.

Selle d'Agneau au Romarin

1 saddle of lamb (1.5-1.75 kg/3½-4 lb, when trimmed)
salt and freshly ground black pepper
12 sprigs fresh rosemary
olive oil or melted butter

SAUCE
4 sprigs fresh rosemary
150 ml/¼ pint water
150 ml/¼ pint well-flavoured gravy
225 g/8 oz softened butter, diced
2 tablespoons cognac
salt and freshly ground black pepper

1. Preheat oven to very hot (240°C, 475°F, Gas Mark 9).

2. Season saddle of lamb with salt and freshly ground black pepper. Tie 12 sprigs of fresh rosemary to it and sprinkle lightly with olive oil or melted butter.

3. Roast lamb in preheated very hot oven for 15 minutes; reduce heat to moderately hot (200°C, 400°F, Gas Mark 6) and cook for 16 to 20 minutes per half kilo/per lb for pink; 20 to 25 minutes per half kilo/per lb for well-done. Serve with sauce.

4. To make sauce: place rosemary and water in a saucepan and bring to the boil. Reduce water to about 4 tablespoons over a high heat. Heat gravy in the top of a double saucepan, add 2 tablespoons reduced rosemary water to this and then, over hot but not boiling water, beat in diced softened butter until sauce is thick and smooth. Add cognac and salt and freshly ground black pepper to taste.

Rack of Lamb with Harem Pilaff 'Rainbow Room'

2 racks of baby lamb, trimmed
salt and freshly ground black pepper
1 level tablespoon English mustard
3 tablespoons dry white wine
8 level tablespoons fresh breadcrumbs
4 level tablespoons finely chopped parsley
1 level tablespoon finely chopped garlic

HAREM PILAFF
4 level tablespoons finely chopped onion
100 g/4 oz fresh butter
225 g/8 oz rice
4 tablespoons white wine
900 ml/1½ pints beef stock
salt
100 g/4 oz button mushrooms, sliced
100 g/4 oz avocado pear, diced
½ level tablespoon finely chopped garlic
100 g/4 oz tomatoes, peeled, seeded and diced
¼ level teaspoon oregano
salt and freshly ground black pepper
75 g/3 oz raw chicken livers, diced

1. Season trimmed racks of lamb generously with salt and freshly ground black pepper and roast in a moderately hot oven (200°C, 400°F, Gas Mark 6) for 20 minutes.

2. Form a paste with English mustard and dry white wine. Brush racks of lamb with paste, then pat on mixture of breadcrumbs and finely chopped parsley and garlic. Return meat to oven and roast for 8 to 10 minutes. Serve with Harem Pilaff.

3. To make Harem Pilaff: sauté finely chopped onion in half the butter for 1 minute. Add rice and stir for another minute. Pour white wine and beef stock over rice and season with salt. Bring to the boil, cover casserole and let simmer for 18 minutes. Stir once only with a fork. In the meantime, sauté mushrooms in 2 tablespoons butter for 3 minutes then add diced avocado and finely chopped garlic. Sauté for 1 minute, add diced tomatoes and oregano, and season to taste with salt and freshly ground black pepper. Let simmer for 5 minutes. In another pan, sauté chicken livers in remaining butter and add to the finished rice, stirring with a fork.

4. Form rice into a ring, and fill centre with avocado and mushroom mixture.

Roast Leg of Lamb with Rosemary

1 leg of lamb (2.25-2.75 kg/5-6 lb)
2 fat cloves garlic, slivered
1-2 level teaspoons dried rosemary
juice of 1 lemon
6 level tablespoons softened butter
salt and freshly ground black pepper
freshly grated nutmeg

1. Preheat oven to moderately hot (190°C, 375°F, Gas Mark 5).

2. Cut small slits in the lamb and insert slivers of garlic.

3. Combine rosemary with lemon juice, softened butter, salt, freshly ground black pepper and freshly grated nutmeg, to taste. Spread leg of lamb with this mixture and place on a rack in an open roasting tin. Place meat in oven.

4. Reduce oven heat to cool (150°C, 300°F, Gas Mark 2) and roast meat, uncovered, for 20 to 25 minutes per half kilo/per lb.

5. Transfer lamb to a heated serving dish and allow to stand for 20 minutes before carving.

Trader Vic's Indonesian Lamb Roast

39

1 best end of lamb (about 8 ribs)

JAVANESE SATÉ SAUCE
1 large Spanish onion, finely chopped
½ level tablespoon salt
½ level tablespoon garlic salt
pinch of monosodium glutamate
1 level tablespoon Trader Vic's Saté Spice
   (or ½ level tablespoon curry powder and
   ½ level teaspoon each powdered turmeric,
   coriander and chilli powder)
juice of 1 lemon
1-3 level tablespoons honey
freshly ground black pepper

1. Cut best end of lamb into 4 portions. Trim all the fat to the rib bones. Wrap the bone ends with foil to prevent burning.

2. To make sauce: combine all ingredients in a large porcelain bowl.

3. Marinate lamb in Javanese Saté Sauce for at least 12 hours.

4. When ready to serve: barbecue lamb in a moderately hot oven (190°C, 375°F, Gas Mark 5) for 18 to 20 minutes, or until tender. Remove foil and serve.

Lamb's Kidneys en Brochette

8-12 lamb's kidneys
4-6 tablespoons melted butter
salt and freshly ground black pepper
fresh breadcrumbs
garlic butter
4 rashers grilled bacon
sprigs of watercress
boiled new potatoes

1. Split kidneys in half from rounded edge and remove thin outer skin. Open them out and run skewer through them to keep them open.

2. Brush with melted butter, season with salt and freshly ground black pepper, and sprinkle generously with breadcrumbs. Place under a grill and cook for 10 to 15 minutes, until cooked.

3. **Just before serving:** place a knob of garlic butter on each kidney half. Garnish with grilled bacon and watercress. Serve with boiled new potatoes.

Lamb's Kidneys with Port Wine

8-12 lamb's kidneys
butter
½ Spanish onion, finely chopped
4 level tablespoons finely chopped parsley
salt and freshly ground black pepper
4-6 button mushrooms, thinly sliced
1 level teaspoon flour
4-6 tablespoons port
4 croûtons fried in butter, or cooked rice

1. Clean kidneys of fibres and fat and slice thinly

2. Melt 4 level tablespoons butter in a frying pan and add finely chopped onion and parsley. Sauté, stirring constantly, for a few minutes. Season to taste with salt and freshly ground black pepper.

3. Add kidneys and sliced mushrooms and continue to cook, stirring continuously, until tender.

4. Make a *beurre manié* by mashing flour to a smooth paste with 2 level teaspoons butter. Stir *beurre manié* into kidneys, stir in port, and cook, stirring constantly, until well blended. Serve with *croûtons* fried in butter, or cooked rice.

Rognons au Porto 'La Paillote'

4 calf's kidneys
butter
½ Spanish onion, finely chopped
2-4 tablespoons parsley, finely chopped
salt and freshly ground black pepper
4-6 button mushrooms, thinly sliced
1-2 level teaspoons flour
2-4 tablespoons port
baked pastry case or cooked rice

Steps **1** to **3**, as for Lamb's Kidneys with Port Wine.

4. Make a *beurre manié* by mashing flour to a smooth paste with 2 level teaspoons butter. Stir *beurre manié* into kidneys, stir in port and cook, stirring constantly, until well blended. Serve in a baked pastry case or ring of cooked rice.

Rognons Flambés

8-12 lamb's kidneys
6 level tablespoons butter
4 level tablespoons finely chopped onion
1 level tablespoon Dijon mustard
salt and freshly ground black pepper
6 tablespoons port
cognac
4 level tablespoons finely chopped parsley
juice of ½ lemon
boiled new potatoes

1. Remove thin outer skins from kidneys.

2. Sauté quickly in half the butter with finely

chopped onion until kidneys stiffen and begin to brown. Dice kidneys (the interiors will still be raw). Melt remaining butter in a thick-bottomed frying pan and add diced kidneys, onion, Dijon mustard, salt and freshly ground black pepper. Stir over a high heat for a minute or two then add port. Reduce heat and allow to simmer, stirring continuously, until kidneys are tender.

3. Sprinkle kidneys with cognac and ignite, allow the flames to die down, stirring continuously. Do not allow sauce to boil at any time during its preparation, or kidneys will be tough.

4. Just before serving, sprinkle with finely chopped parsley and lemon juice. Serve with boiled new potatoes.

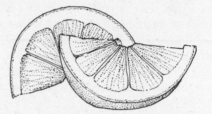

Rognons Sautés au Vin Rouge

8-12 lamb's kidneys
100 g/4 oz mushrooms, sliced
4 level tablespoons butter
1 Spanish onion, finely chopped
150 ml/¼ pint red wine
4 level tablespoons Demi-glace or Brown Sauce (see page 83)
2-4 level tablespoons finely chopped parsley

1. Sauté sliced mushrooms in butter until golden, remove and keep warm.

2. Sauté chopped onion in pan until transparent, add kidneys, cut in small pieces, and simmer lightly for a minute or two. Pour red wine over meat and cook, stirring until sauce bubbles.

3. Reduce heat, stir in Demi-glace or Brown Sauce, and allow to simmer for a minute, until reduced to half the original quantity.

4. Stir in cooked mushrooms, sprinkle with parsley and serve.

41

42

Spiedini di Vitello alla Romana
Illustrated on page 27

4 thin veal escalopes
4 slices prosciutto (Parma ham)
4 slices Parmesan or Gruyère cheese
salt and freshly ground black pepper
unsliced bread
butter
olive oil
dry vermouth or dry white wine
shredded lettuce

1. Place each piece of veal between 2 sheets of waxed paper and flatten them with a wooden mallet, or with the flat side of a cleaver.

2. Place a thin slice of *prosciutto* (Parma ham) and a thin slice of Parmesan or Gruyère cheese on each escalope. Season to taste with salt and freshly ground black pepper, and roll up.

3. Cut 6 cubes of bread from a whole loaf approximately to the size of the meat rolls. Trim crusts.

4. Spear a piece of bread on a metal skewer; add a veal roll, then a piece of bread, then another veal roll, and finally a piece of bread.

5. When ready to serve, sauté the skewered *spiedini* in butter with just a little olive oil for about 10 minutes. When the meat begins to take on a little colour, add a little dry vermouth or white wine to the pan and allow to sizzle for a few minutes. Serve on a bed of shredded lettuce or Saffron Rice.

Saffron Rice

1 level tablespoon butter
1 Spanish onion
225 g/8 oz rice
150 ml/¼ pint chicken stock, strained
salt and freshly ground black pepper
freshly grated nutmeg
generous pinch saffron

1. Melt butter in a saucepan; add finely chopped onion and stir over the heat until transparent.

2. Stir in rice. Add strained chicken stock and salt, freshly ground black pepper, a little freshly grated nutmeg and saffron, to taste, and simmer gently, covered, for about 25 minutes, or until rice is tender but not mushy.

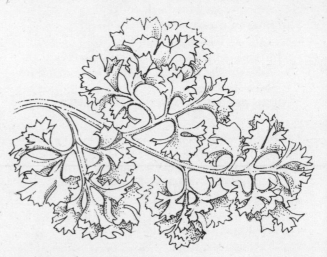

Medaillons de Veau 'Orloff'

6 slices fillet of veal (about 100 g/4 oz each)
salt and freshly ground black pepper
flour
butter
6 shallots
8 tablespoons dry white wine
8 tablespoons port
8 tablespoons stock

1. Season fillets with salt and freshly ground black pepper and dust them lightly with flour. Sear on both sides in a shallow pan containing 4 tablespoons melted butter. Lower the heat and cook slowly for 10 to 12 minutes. Remove from pan and keep hot.

2. Chop the shallots and soften them in the pan juices, add the white wine and port. Reduce by half over a high heat and add the stock.

3. When hot but not boiling, remove from the heat and stir in 2 to 4 tablespoons butter in small pieces. Pour sauce over the steaks. Serve immediately.

Côtes de Veau Grandmère 'Petite Auberge' *Serves 4*
Sweetbreads à la Royale *Serves 4*
Costolette di Vitello alla Valdostana *Serves 6*

Côtes de Veau Grandmère 'Petite Auberge'

4 thick veal chops
salt and freshly ground black pepper
2 level tablespoons butter
2 tablespoons olive oil
16 button onions
100 g/4 oz bacon, diced
8 button mushrooms, cut in quarters
4 tablespoons well-flavoured beef stock or glace de viande
2-4 level tablespoons finely chopped parsley

1. Season veal chops to taste with salt and freshly ground black pepper, and sauté in butter and olive oil until golden on both sides. Cover pan and simmer chops gently for about 10 minutes.

2. Place button onions and diced bacon in cold water and bring to the boil. Drain, and add to chops with quartered mushrooms. Simmer gently, uncovered, for about 5 minutes. Add well-flavoured beef stock or *glace de viande*. Sprinkle with finely chopped parsley and serve immediately.

Sweetbreads à la Royale

2 pairs sweetbreads
salt
juice of $\frac{1}{2}$ lemon
1 Spanish onion, coarsely chopped
2 carrots, coarsely chopped
butter
2 level tablespoons flour
freshly ground black pepper
4 tablespoons cognac
8 tablespoons dry white wine
150 ml/$\frac{1}{4}$ pint well-flavoured chicken stock
2 tablespoons double cream
8 tablespoons port
4 mushroom caps, sautéed in butter

1. Soak sweetbreads in cold water for 1 hour, changing water when it becomes tinged with pink. Blanch them for 15 minutes in simmering salted water to which you have added lemon juice. Drain and cool, then trim and cut into slices 5 cm/2 inches thick.

2. Sauté chopped onion and carrots in a little butter until golden. Remove and keep warm.

3. Flour sweetbreads lightly, add to pan with a little more butter and sauté until golden. Spoon vegetables over sweetbreads, season to taste with salt and freshly ground black pepper. Cover with buttered paper and place in a moderately hot oven (190°C, 375°F, Gas Mark 5) for 10 minutes. Remove paper, flame with heated cognac and remove sweetbreads to a heated serving dish. Keep warm.

4. Add dry white wine to the pan and cook over a high heat, stirring continuously and scraping all crusty bits from sides of pan, until sauce is reduced to half the original quantity. Add chicken stock and simmer gently for 5 minutes, strain then add cream and port. Correct seasoning and pour sauce over sweetbreads. Top with sautéed mushroom caps.

Costolette di Vitello alla Valdostana

6 large veal cutlets
175 g/6 oz Fontina cheese, thinly sliced
canned white truffles, thinly sliced
salt and freshly ground black pepper
flour
2 eggs, beaten
breadcrumbs
butter
1 tablespoon olive oil
boiled rice
freshly grated Parmesan cheese

1. Slice the cutlets with a sharp knife to make a pocket with both parts still attached to the bone. Stuff this pocket with thin slices of Fontina cheese and white truffle. Season to taste with salt and freshly ground black pepper. Press the pocket shut, beating the edges to seal them properly.

2. Flour the cutlets, roll them in beaten egg and then in breadcrumbs. Sauté cutlets gently in 3 tablespoons butter and 1 tablespoon olive oil until they are a rich golden brown. Serve with boiled rice dressed with butter and freshly grated Parmesan.

43

Veal Parmesan 'Four Seasons' *Serves 8*
Veal Medaillons with Pommes de Terre Macaire
Serves 4 to 6
Veal Chops aux Fines Herbes *Serves 4 to 6*

44

Veal Parmesan 'Four Seasons'

16 thin escalopes of veal
flour
3 eggs, well beaten
100 g/4 oz fresh breadcrumbs
225 g/8 oz freshly grated Parmesan cheese
grated rind of 5 lemons
olive oil or butter

1. Dip thin slices of veal in flour, then in beaten egg, and finally in a mixture of breadcrumbs, Parmesan and lemon rind.

2. Sauté veal slices on both sides in oil or butter until golden brown. Serve immediately.

Veal Medaillons with Pommes de Terre Macaire

4-6 veal chops
salt and freshly ground black pepper
flour
4 level tablespoons butter
1 tablespoon olive oil
4-6 tablespoons port
stock (see method)
4 level tablespoons sultanas

POMMES DE TERRE MACAIRE
1 kg/2 lb medium-sized potatoes
175 g/6 oz softened butter
salt and freshly ground black pepper

1. **To make Pommes de Terre Macaire:** bake potatoes in a moderately hot oven (200°C, 400°F, Gas Mark 6) for 40 to 50 minutes. Cut them in half and scoop out the pulp. Using a fork, mash this pulp up with the softened butter. Season generously with salt and freshly ground black pepper. Spread mixture in well-buttered individual patty tins just the size of the *medaillons* (see below). Return to the oven and bake for 25 to 30 minutes to form well-browned potato cakes.

Note: potato cakes can be kept warm in a low oven while you prepare *medaillons*.

2. Trim bones from veal chops to make veal

rounds. Season veal rounds with salt and freshly ground black pepper, dust with flour and sauté in butter and olive oil until tender.

3. Remove veal and keep warm, pour off excess butter and add port and a little well-flavoured stock (made with veal bones, 1 bay leaf, ½ chicken stock cube and a little water), stirring in all the crusty bits from the sides of the pan.

4. **To serve:** unmould potato cakes on to a heated serving dish, top with veal *medaillons* and mask with port sauce in which you have heated some sultanas, previously soaked overnight in a little port. Serve immediately.

Veal Chops aux Fines Herbes

4-6 veal chops
salt and freshly ground black pepper
butter
2 tablespoons olive oil
6 tablespoons dry white wine
2 level tablespoons finely chopped shallots, or onion
150 ml/¼ pint well-flavoured veal or chicken stock
1 level tablespoon flour
2 level tablespoons mixed fines herbes (parsley, chervil and tarragon), finely chopped

1. Season veal chops generously with salt and freshly ground black pepper. Sauté gently on both sides in 2 tablespoons each butter and olive oil until almost tender.

2. Add dry white wine and finely chopped shallots or onion, and continue cooking until done. Transfer to a heated serving dish and keep warm.

3. Reduce dry white wine and pan juices over a high heat to half of the original quantity. Heat the well-flavoured stock, thicken with a *beurre marie* made by mashing together 1 tablespoon each butter and flour and add to the pan juices. Stir in finely chopped *fines herbes* and pour over chops. Serve immediately.

Carré d'Agneau Persillé (see page 36)

Crown Roast of Lamb (see page 37)

Lamb and Bacon Kebabs (see page 36)

Grilled Lamb Chops (see page 35)

Italian Veal Cutlets au Gratin

8 thin escalopes of veal
150 ml/¼ pint double cream
4 level tablespoons freshly grated Parmesan
   cheese
100 g/4 oz Mozzarella cheese, diced
100 g/4 oz cooked ham, diced
2 eggs
salt and freshly ground black pepper
2 level tablespoons butter
2 tablespoons oil

1. Combine cream, grated Parmesan and diced Mozzarella cheese and ham in the top of a double saucepan. Cook over hot water, stirring constantly until cheese melts.

2. Beat eggs in a bowl, then whisk in hot cheese mixture and season to taste with salt and freshly ground black pepper.

3. Melt butter and oil in a thick-bottomed frying pan and brown veal escalopes on both sides. Season with salt and freshly ground black pepper. Place 2 escalopes in each of 4 individual *gratin* dishes and spoon cheese mixture over them. Grill until sauce is well browned and bubbling.

Noix de Veau Farcie

1 noix de veau (a piece of topside of leg or
   rump), trimmed of fat, boned and rolled
   into a compact shape 10-14 cm/4-5½
   inches in diameter, about 1.5 kg/3 lb
salt and freshly ground black pepper
crushed rosemary
softened butter
8 button mushroom caps, sliced
450 ml/¾ pint Sauce Suprême (see page 84)
4-6 level tablespoons freshly grated
   Parmesan cheese
4 thin slices pâté de foie gras, diced
thin slices of white truffle
melted butter

1. Season veal with salt, freshly ground black pepper and crushed rosemary. Spread meat with softened butter and roast in a moderately hot

oven (190°C, 375°F, Gas Mark 5) for about 18 to 20 minutes per half kilo/per lb, basting frequently. Add a little hot water if fat tends to scorch.

2. Cut a thin slice off the top of the meat and then carefully cut out the interior with a sharp knife (as you would for a *brioche farcie* or a *vol-au-vent*), leaving a thin shell of meat.

3. Slice veal taken from *noix* into thin strips or scallops, and sauté for a few minutes in butter with sliced mushrooms. Add 300 ml/½ pint Sauce Suprême flavoured with freshly grated Parmesan, and fold in diced *pâté de foi gras* and sliced truffle.

4. Fill the meat shell with this mixture, replace the cover and brush with melted butter. Return to the oven for several minutes to glaze. Serve immediately with remaining Sauce Suprême.

Roast Loin of Veal

1 loin of veal (1.5 kg/3 lb when boned,
   rolled and tied)
salt and freshly ground black pepper
4 level tablespoons softened butter
crushed rosemary
crumbled bay leaves
150 ml/¼ pint dry white wine
1 level tablespoon tomato purée

1. Ask your butcher to bone, trim and tie a loin of veal. Season loin of veal to taste with salt and freshly ground black pepper. Spread with softened butter and sprinkle with crushed rosemary and crumbled bay leaves. Roast the meat in a moderate oven (160°C, 325°F, Gas Mark 3) for about 30 minutes per half kilo/per lb, or until juices run clear, basting frequently. The meat should be moist but not pink. Add a little hot water if fat tends to scorch during cooking.

2. Remove veal from oven and skim excess fat from juices left in roasting tin. Add dry white wine and tomato purée to pan juices and cook on top of the cooker, scraping bottom and sides of tin with a wooden spoon to dislodge any crusty morsels stuck there. Allow to simmer for 2 to 3 minutes. Correct seasoning, strain and serve with the roast.

Danish Meat Balls (Frikadeller) *Serves 4 to 6*
Italian Roast Leg of Veal *Serves 6 to 8*
Roast Loin of Veal with Breadcrumbs *Serves 6*

50

Danish Meat Balls (Frikadeller)

350 g/12 oz finely ground veal
225 g/8 oz finely ground pork
100 g/4 oz flour
450 ml/¾ pint milk
1 egg, beaten
salt and freshly ground black pepper
½ level teaspoon ground cloves
1 medium-sized onion, finely chopped and
    sautéed in butter
butter and oil for frying

1. Combine finely ground meats and flour, mixing well. Add milk little by little, stirring well to make a smooth paste. Stir in egg and season to taste with salt, freshly ground black pepper, ground cloves, and finely chopped onion which you have sautéed in butter until transparent.

2. Form mixture into small balls about 2.5 cm/1 inch in diameter and fry *frikadeller* evenly on all sides in butter and oil until cooked through.

Italian Roast Leg of Veal

1 leg of veal (2-2.75 kg/4½-6 lb), boned and
    tied
salt and freshly ground black pepper
dried thyme
225 g/8 oz unsmoked bacon, thinly sliced
2 cloves garlic
4 carrots, thinly sliced
1 Spanish onion, thinly sliced
2 bay leaves
100 g/4 oz butter
300 ml/½ pint dry white wine
2-3 level tablespoons tomato purée
beurre manié (see method)

1. Lard the veal with fat and tie it securely into a neat roast.

2. Two hours before cooking veal, remove it from refrigerator. Rub meat with salt, freshly ground black pepper and dried thyme, and allow meat to absorb flavour for a minimum of 2 hours.

3. When ready to cook veal, cover meat with thin bacon slices and put it in a roasting tin. Surround veal with garlic cloves, sliced carrots, onion and bay leaves. Melt the butter, combine with wine and tomato purée and pour over meat. Roast in a moderate oven (160°C, 325°F, Gas Mark 3) for 20 minutes per half kilo/per lb or until veal is well-done but juicy, basting frequently.

3. Skim fat from surface of pan juices and thicken gravy slightly with a *beurre manié*, made by mashing together 1 tablespoon each butter and flour.

Roast Loin of Veal with Breadcrumbs

1 loin of veal (1.5 kg/3 lb when boned,
    rolled and tied)
6 rashers unsmoked bacon
4 level tablespoons softened butter
1 Spanish onion, finely chopped
2 carrots, finely chopped
2 sticks celery, finely chopped
salt and freshly ground black pepper
450 ml/¾ pint well-flavoured stock
1 egg, well beaten
6-8 level tablespoons breadcrumbs
2-4 level tablespoons freshly grated
    Parmesan cheese

1. Line roasting tin with rashers of bacon and place rolled veal on the bacon. Spread meat with softened butter and surround it with chopped onion, carrots and celery. Season meat generously with salt and freshly ground black pepper, and roast in a hot oven (230°C, 450°F, Gas Mark 8) until well browned on all sides.

2. Add stock, reduce oven heat to cool (150°C, 300°F, Gas Mark 2) and continue roasting the meat for 1½ to 2 hours, until it is cooked, basting frequently.

3. Remove strings from roast, and brush top and sides with egg. Sprinkle with breadcrumbs and Parmesan and return to the oven for 15 minutes, or until crumbs are golden.

4. Reduce pan juices over high heat, strain and serve with roast.

Liver

Swiss Liver Brochettes

4-6 thin slices fresh calf's liver
16 sage leaves
6 level tablespoons butter
2 tablespoons olive oil
½ Spanish onion, finely chopped
4-6 potatoes
salt and freshly ground black pepper

1. Cut thin slices of liver into 20 even-sized rect-angles. Place each rectangle alternately with sage leaf on metal skewers, allowing 5 liver pieces to each skewer. Heat a little butter and olive oil in a thick-bottomed frying pan, and sauté finely chopped onion until transparent. Add liver *broch-ettes* and sauté, covered, until brown and tender.

2. Peel potatoes and grate coarsely.

3. Heat remaining butter and oil in frying pan. (I like to use an oval pan for this recipe as the *broch-ettes* look so attractive on an oval potato cake.) Add potatoes and season generously with salt and freshly ground black pepper. Simmer gently, covered, shaking pan from time to time to prevent sticking, until potato cake is crisp and brown on the bottom. Invert potato cake on to a plate and then slide cake into frying pan to brown other side.

4. **To serve:** arrange the *brochettes* on the potato cake.

Le Foie Chaud Pommes

675 g/1½ lb fresh calf's liver, sliced
1 kg/2 lb tart eating apples, cored, peeled
   and quartered
1 glass white Alsatian wine
100 g/4 oz dried currants, soaked in wine
¼ teaspoon cinnamon
salt and freshly ground black pepper
pinch of ground cloves
pinch of powdered thyme
1 level tablespoon flour
4 level tablespoons butter
finely chopped parsley

1. Simmer peeled and quartered apples in white Alsatian wine until tender. Add the currants, which you have soaked in wine, and the cinnamon and keep warm.

2. Season sliced liver with salt, freshly ground black pepper, ground cloves and powdered thyme. Sprinkle with flour, and brown in butter for 3 minutes.

3. Arrange the *compote* of warm apples on a heated serving dish, place sautéed liver slices on top and garnish with finely chopped parsley.

Calf's Liver with Avocado 'Four Seasons'

12 thin slices calf's liver
2-3 avocado pears
juice of three lemons
flour
salt and freshly ground black pepper
225 g/8 oz butter
8 tablespoons beef or veal stock
½ level teaspoon thyme

1. Peel avocados, remove stones and cut thinly into 12 slices. Brush each slice with a little lemon juice to preserve colour.

2. Slice calf's liver thinly.

3. Dip sliced avocado and calf's liver in flour well seasoned with salt and freshly ground black pepper. Sauté very quickly in a little butter. Arrange on platter.

4. Brown remaining butter in saucepan, add remaining lemon juice, beef or veal stock and thyme. Pour over liver.

51

52

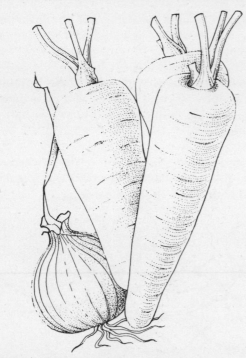

Pork Chops in Red Wine

4-6 good-sized pork chops
salt and freshly ground black pepper
flour
2 level tablespoons butter
2 tablespoons olive oil
4 level tablespoons finely chopped shallots,
  or onion
150 ml/¼ pint red wine
2-4 level tablespoons finely chopped parsley

1. Trim excess fat from pork chops and season them generously with salt and freshly ground black pepper. Dust with flour and sauté gently in butter and olive oil until brown on both sides.

2. Transfer the pork chops to a heated serving dish, pouring off excess fat from pan. Add finely chopped shallots, or onion, and red wine to the pan and cook slowly, stirring in all the crusty bits from sides and bottom of the pan. Skim fat and cook sauce until reduced to half of the original quantity.

3. Correct seasoning and pour over chops. Sprinkle with finely chopped parsley and serve immediately.

Pork Chops 'Avesnoise'

4 thick pork chops, cut from the loin
2 tablespoons olive oil
2 level tablespoons butter
salt and freshly ground black pepper
100 g/4 oz Gruyère cheese, freshly grated
1-2 level teaspoons Dijon mustard
double cream

1. Trim excess fat from 4 good-sized pork chops and sauté them gently with a little oil and butter in a thick-bottomed frying pan. Season to taste with salt and freshly ground black pepper.

2. When cooked, remove from pan and allow to cool. Make a *pommade* of finely grated Gruyère (about 6 tablespoons) mixed with mustard and just enough double cream to make a smooth mixture of spreading consistency. Place chops on a grill pan and spread generously with cheese *pommade*. Glaze quickly under the grill until cheese mixture is bubbling and golden. Serve immediately.

Indonesian Skewered Pork

1.5-kg/3 lb loin of pork, boned but not tied
salt and freshly ground black pepper
2 level teaspoons coriander
2 level teaspoons cumin seed
1 Spanish onion, finely chopped
2 level teaspoons brown sugar
4 tablespoons soy sauce
4 tablespoons lemon juice
¼ level teaspoon powdered ginger

1. Cut pork into 2.5-cm/1-inch cubes and combine in a porcelain bowl with remaining ingredients. Mix well and allow pork cubes to marinate in this mixture for at least 4 hours, turning from time to time so that it becomes impregnated with all the flavours.

2. **When ready to grill:** drain and reserve marinade. Arrange 4 to 6 cubes of meat on each skewer, brush with marinade and grill for 5 minutes. Turn pork and baste with marinade every 5 minutes until pork is done – 20 to 25 minutes in all.

Roast Loin of Pork Normande

1 loin of pork (7-8 cutlets)
salt and freshly ground black pepper
dried thyme
freshly grated nutmeg
4-6 tablespoons apple cider
4-6 level tablespoons apple jelly
flour and butter
watercress
4 eating apples, cored and thinly sliced,
sautéed in 4 level tablespoons butter

1. Rub pork with salt, freshly ground black pepper, thyme, and a sprinkling of nutmeg. Arrange meat fat side up and brown in a hot oven (230°C, 450°F, Gas Mark 8) for 10 minutes. Reduce heat to moderate (180°C, 350°F, Gas Mark 4) and continue to roast until meat is cooked, basting with blended cider and jelly for the first $1\frac{1}{2}$ hours of cooking time.

2. Remove excess fat from the pan, adding a little water or cider if fat starts to scorch. Make gravy by thickening pan drippings with a little flour kneaded with an equal amount of butter. Serve with watercress and thinly sliced sautéed apples.

Roast Loin of Pork
Illustrated on page 27

1 loin of pork (7-8 cutlets)
1-2 cloves garlic, cut in slivers
2-3 bay leaves, crumbled
6 level tablespoons softened butter
crumbled thyme and rosemary
Dijon mustard
salt and freshly ground black pepper
flour
butter
watercress
puréed potatoes

1. Ask your butcher to remove rind from pork without removing fat.

2. Make incisions the length of the loin, near the bone, with a sharp knife. Insert a sliver of garlic and a segment of bay leaf into each incision.

3. Mix softened butter, crumbled thyme, rosemary and mustard, to taste, into a smooth paste, and rub well into pork several hours before roasting. Season to taste with salt and freshly ground black pepper, and let stand at room temperature to absorb flavours.

4. Arrange the meat fat side up and brown in a hot oven (230°C, 450°F, Gas Mark 8) for 15 minutes. Reduce the oven heat to moderate (180°C, 350°F, Gas Mark 4) and continue to roast until the meat is cooked.

5. Remove excess fat from the pan and thicken pan drippings with a little flour kneaded with an equal amount of butter. Garnish with sprigs of watercress, and serve with puréed potatoes.

Chinese Fried Pork Pellets

450 g/1 lb pork fillet
$\frac{1}{2}$ teaspoon salt
pinch of monosodium glutamate
1-2 tablespoons sake or dry sherry
corn or peanut oil for frying

BATTER
1 egg white
6 level tablespoons cornflour
3 tablespoons soy sauce
2 tablespoons sake
2 teaspoons ginger syrup

1. Cut pork into bite-sized pieces, place in a bowl and season with salt, monosodium glutamate and *sake* or dry sherry.

2. To make batter: beat egg white in a bowl until stiff, add cornflour mixed with soy sauce, *sake* and ginger juice, and mix well to make batter.

3. Heat oil for deep-frying to 180°C/350°F.

4. Coat pork well with batter and fry until crisp and golden.

Serves 4, if served with two or more other Chinese dishes. Double quantities if served alone as a main course.

53

Chinese Pork with Watercress *Serves 2 to 3*
Filet de Porc en Croûte *Serves 4*
Roast Loin of Pork Boulangère (High Heat Method)
Serves 4

54

Chinese Pork with Watercress

4 bunches watercress
1 level teaspoon salt
juice of ½ lemon
4 tablespoons corn oil
1 small clove garlic, finely chopped
450 g/1 lb fillet of pork, thinly sliced
2-3 tablespoons soy sauce
1 tablespoon sake or dry sherry

1. Trim watercress stems and wash well, picking out any yellowed or damaged leaves. Drain. Soak for 30 minutes in cold water to which you have added salt and lemon juice. Drain, rinse in clean water and dry.

2. **When ready to serve:** heat oil in frying pan, add garlic and thin pork slices, and brown the meat quickly on all sides. Add the soy sauce, *sake* or dry sherry, and watercress, and cook, stirring constantly, until the juices begin to boil. Cover pan and cook for 2 minutes longer. Serve immediately.
Serves 4 to 6, if served with two or more other Chinese dishes.

Filet de Porc en Croûte

1 fillet of pork (about 400-450 g/14-16 oz)
salt and freshly ground black pepper
Puff Pastry (see page 91)
50 g/2 oz Parma ham, sliced very thinly
beaten egg

DUXELLES
450 g/1 lb button mushrooms, finely
  chopped
1 Spanish onion, finely chopped
4 level tablespoons butter
salt and freshly ground black pepper
powdered thyme
2-3 level tablespoons freshly chopped
  parsley
4-6 level tablespoons fresh breadcrumbs
2 eggs, well beaten

1. Season fillet lightly with salt and freshly ground black pepper, and seal it quickly on all sides. Cool.

2. **To make duxelles:** sauté finely chopped mushrooms and onion in butter, season to taste with salt, freshly ground black pepper and powdered thyme. Add freshly chopped parsley and fresh breadcrumbs. Stir in beaten eggs, mix well and heat through. Turn out into a small pan and set aside to cool.

Note: This filling should be prepared in advance.

3. Roll out puff pastry about 3 mm/⅛ inch thick, in a shape 5 cm/2 inches longer than the fillet and about 25 cm/10 inches wide. Place fillet in centre of pastry, spread evenly with the *duxelles* and top with thin slices of ham. Fold one side of pastry over the pork, spread a little beaten egg over the upper surface and then fold over the second side of the pastry, overlapping the first. Roll pastry ends out flat, spread with beaten egg on the upper side and fold the ends over the roll. Place pastry-wrapped fillet in a baking tin with the folded ends down. Brush the surface with beaten egg and decorate with lattice strips of leaves cut from pastry scraps. Brush pastry again with beaten egg and prick lightly with a fork. Bake in a moderately hot oven (200°C, 400°F, Gas Mark 6) for about 40 minutes.

Roast Loin of Pork Boulangère (High Heat Method)

1 loin of pork (7-8 cutlets)
salt and freshly ground black pepper
butter
2 level tablespoons flour
6-8 large potatoes
1 Spanish onion, finely chopped
2-4 level tablespoons finely chopped parsley
hot light stock or water

1. Season pork generously with salt and freshly ground black pepper and place it on the rack of a roasting tin. Roast in a hot oven (220°C, 425°F, Gas Mark 7) for 1 hour, or until pork is half cooked, basting from time to time.

2. Remove pork and roasting rack from tin and skim off excess fat. Thicken pan gravy with a *beurre manié* of 2 level tablespoons each butter and

flour mashed together to a smooth paste. Pour into a small saucepan and reserve.

3. Peel and slice potatoes thinly, and place them in roasting tin with finely chopped onion, parsley, salt and freshly ground black pepper, to taste. Spread potatoes with 4 tablespoons softened butter, and place pork roast on top, adding just enough hot stock (or water) to cover the potatoes. Bring the liquid to the boil, return roasting tin to a moderately hot oven (200°C, 400°F, Gas Mark 6) and cook for 1 to 1½ hours longer, until meat is done. The liquid should almost have completely cooked away, and the potatoes nicely browned on top.

4. Reheat pan gravy and serve with roast potatoes.

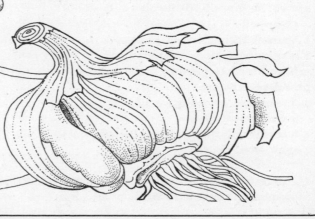

Barbecued Loin of Pork

1 loin of pork
¼ level teaspoon dry mustard
¼ level teaspoon ground coriander
¼ level teaspoon ground cloves
2 cloves garlic, finely chopped
¼ level teaspoon freshly ground black pepper
4 tablespoons olive oil
4 tablespoons soy sauce
4 tablespoons vinegar
6 tablespoons water
2 level tablespoons sugar
1 small fresh pineapple

GARNISH
diced fresh pineapple
sliced cucumber
watercress and parsley sprigs

1. Ask your butcher to cut backbone from ribs.

2. Mix mustard, coriander, cloves, garlic, freshly ground black pepper, olive oil, soy sauce, vinegar, water and sugar together in a saucepan. Bring to the boil, lower the heat and simmer for 30 minutes.

3. Peel pineapple, reserving flesh for garnish. Place loin in a roasting tin, brush with marinade and cover with pineapple skin. Roast meat in a moderate oven (180°C, 350°F, Gas Mark 4) for about 2 hours, or until cooked, basting frequently with hot barbecue sauce.

4. Garnish with diced fresh pineapple, sliced cucumber, watercress and parsley sprigs.

Roast Leg of Pork Cooked Like Game
Jambon à la Crème du Relais Fleuri *Serves 4*
Ham Steaks 'Forum of the Twelve Caesars' *Serves 6*

56

Roast Leg of Pork Cooked Like Game

Illustrated on page 26

1 leg of pork
olive oil
2 Spanish onions, thinly sliced
4 cloves garlic, thinly sliced
1 bottle red Burgundy
peel of 1 orange
300 ml/½ pint chicken stock

AROMATIC SPICE MIXTURE
1 level teaspoon salt
½ level teaspoon powdered nutmeg
¼ level teaspoon powdered cloves
2 bay leaves, crumbled
½ level teaspoon thyme
12 peppercorns, crushed

1. Ask your butcher to trim a leg of fresh pork to the shape of a ham, and to score the fat.

2. Rub the pork with olive oil and then with aromatic spice mixture. Place pork on a serving dish large enough to hold it, and keep in refrigerator for 24 hours to allow flavours to permeate meat.

3. Remove pork from refrigerator; place it in a large deep container with sliced onions and garlic, red wine, 150 ml/¼ pint olive oil, orange peel and chicken stock. Marinate pork in this mixture for 3 to 4 days, turning the meat in the marinade twice each day.

4. Preheat oven to moderate (160°C, 325°F, Gas Mark 3). When ready to cook roast, remove pork from marinade (reserve marinade for later use) and pat meat dry with absorbent paper. Sprinkle with olive oil and place meat on rack in roasting tin. Roast for 25 minutes per half kilo/per lb, or until the meat is cooked through.

5. To make sauce: cook reserved marinade juices over a high heat until reduced by half; strain into a bowl and serve with meat.

6. Transfer meat to a heated platter and keep warm. Strain pan juices into sauce.

Jambon à la Crème du Relais Fleuri

4 thick slices cooked ham
2 level tablespoons butter
2 level tablespoons flour
150 ml/¼ pint port
150 ml/¼ pint chicken stock
freshly ground black pepper
1 egg yolk
150 ml/¼ pint thick cream
salt
2 level tablespoons finely chopped parsley

1. To prepare cream sauce: make a *roux blond* with butter and flour. Add port, chicken stock and freshly ground black pepper, to taste. Simmer until sauce is reduced and is rich and thick. Remove from heat and cool. When sauce is barely warm, combine egg yolk and cream and whisk into sauce. Correct seasoning, adding salt and more pepper, if necessary.

2. Warm ham in a cool oven (150°C, 300°F, Gas Mark 2) for 15 to 20 minutes.

3. When ready to serve: heat sauce, but do not allow to come to the boil, as it will curdle.

4. To serve: arrange ham slices on a warm serving dish and pour sauce over them. Sprinkle with chopped parsley and serve immediately.

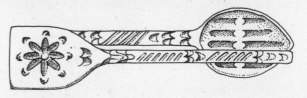

Ham Steaks 'Forum of the Twelve Caesars'

4-6 thick slices ham (about 225 g/8 oz each)
450 g/1 lb Italian spiced mustard fruit (frutta di Cremona)
300 ml/½ pint clear honey, heated
12 walnuts

1. Grill ham steaks on one side for about 3 minutes. Turn and grill other side for 1½ minutes.

2. Arrange segments of mustard fruit on top of steaks and place under grill for 1 to 2 minutes more. Remove from grill, place steaks on a heated serving dish and pour heated honey over them. Garnish each steak with 2 or 3 walnuts. Serve immediately.

Ham Steaks Stuffed with Sweet Potatoes

4 thick slices ham (about 225 g/8 oz each)
1 (425-g/15-oz) can sweet potatoes
4 tablespoons melted butter
grated rind of ½ lemon
grated rind of ½ orange
¼ level teaspoon powdered cinnamon
2–4 tablespoons bourbon or rum
salt and freshly ground black pepper
2–4 level tablespoons brown sugar

1. Mash sweet potatoes with melted butter and flavour with grated lemon and orange rind, cinnamon, bourbon or rum, salt and freshly ground black pepper, to taste.

2. Spread the stuffing thickly on 2 ham steaks and top with remaining steaks. Sprinkle the steaks with a little brown sugar and season with freshly ground black pepper. Wrap loosely in foil and bake in a moderate oven (160°C, 325°F, Gas Mark 3) for 1 hour.

Sausages and Mash

450 g/1 lb pork sausages
2–4 level tablespoons lard
butter
salt and freshly ground black pepper
¼ level teaspoon powdered thyme
¼ level teaspoon powdered sage
2 egg yolks
milk or single cream
675 g/1½ lb potatoes, cooked and mashed
beaten egg (optional)
2–4 tablespoons breadcrumbs

1. Blanch sausages by putting them in a saucepan with cold water and bringing them quickly to

the boil. Drain, remove their skins and cut each one into 3 pieces. Sauté pieces in lard for a minute or two to brown them.

2. Place sausages in a buttered pie dish or oven-proof baking dish and sprinkle them with salt, freshly ground black pepper, powdered thyme and powdered sage.

3. Combine yolks with 4 tablespoons milk or cream, and beat into potato mixture. Season to taste with salt and freshly ground black pepper.

4. Spread potato mixture over sausages. Brush with milk or beaten egg, sprinkle with bread-crumbs and bake in a moderately hot oven (190°C, 375°F, Gas Mark 5) for 20 to 30 minutes, until potatoes are golden brown.

Boiled Salt Pork

1.25 kg–1.5 kg/2½–3 lb pickled or salted pork
2 Spanish onions
6 carrots
12 parsnips or 6 turnips

1. Choose a nice piece of pickled pork or salted pork. Wash it, cover with cold water and soak for 24 hours, changing water several times.

2. When ready to cook, place meat in a saucepan with enough warm water to cover it. Bring slowly to the boil, skim well and then simmer gently until tender, allowing 25 minutes per half kilo/per lb and 25 minutes over.

3. After skimming, add onions, carrots, and parsnips or young turnips.

4. When ready to serve: place the meat on a hot serving dish, strain some of the liquid around it and garnish with vegetables. Use remaining liquid to make pear or lentil soup.

57

Poultry

58

Basic Boiled Chicken

1 boiling chicken, cleaned and trussed
½ lemon
butter
salted water or stock
1 Spanish onion stuck with cloves
2 carrots
2 sticks celery
1 bay leaf
300 ml/½ pint English Parsley Sauce (see
    page 89) or Chicken Velouté Sauce (see
    page 82) or Celery Sauce (see page 84)
bacon rolls or quartered hard-boiled eggs

1. Rub cleaned and trussed boiling chicken with
the cut side of the lemon half and wrap it in a
piece of well-buttered waxed paper to keep it a
good colour.

2. Put the chicken in boiling salted water, or
better yet, a little light stock, with 1 Spanish onion
stuck with cloves, carrots, celery and bay leaf.
Bring to the boil and allow it to simmer slowly
until tender from 2 to 3 hours, depending on age
and size of chicken. Unless cooked slowly, the
flesh will become hard and tasteless.

3. When chicken is tender, remove from stock to a
hot dish. Remove paper and string from chicken,
and mask it with English Parsley, Chicken
Velouté or Celery Sauce. Garnish with little rolls
of bacon or quartered hard-boiled eggs.

Basic Steamed Chicken

1 roasting chicken
½ lemon
salt and freshly ground black pepper
4 tablespoons melted butter
4 tablespoons chicken stock
2 tablespoons finely chopped onion
English Parsley Sauce (see page 89) or
    Velouté Sauce (see page 82) or Celery
    Sauce (see page 84)

1. Rub cleaned and trussed chicken with cut side of
½ lemon and sprinkle with salt and freshly ground
black pepper, to taste. Place it in a *gratin* dish just
large enough to hold it and add butter, chicken
stock and finely chopped onion. Place *gratin* dish
in a large double steamer over 7.5 cm/3 inches of
rapidly boiling water. Cover tightly and steam
for 1 to 2 hours, depending on size of chicken.
Serve with Parsley, Velouté or Celery Sauce.

Chicken Baked in Salt
Illustrated on page 87

1 tender roasting chicken (about 1.5 kg/3 lb
    when dressed)
1.75 kg/4 lb coarse sea salt
softened butter or olive oil
salt and freshly ground black pepper

STUFFING
chicken liver
100 g/4 oz bacon
100 g/4 oz fresh pork
2 cloves garlic, finely chopped
100 g/4 oz dried breadcrumbs
milk or stock, to moisten
4 level tablespoons finely chopped parsley
½ level teaspoon dried tarragon
generous pinch of mixed spice
salt and freshly ground black pepper
butter
2 eggs

1. To make stuffing: put chicken liver, bacon,
fresh pork and garlic through the finest blade of
your mincer. Moisten breadcrumbs with a little
milk or stock; combine with minced meats and
add finely chopped parsley, dried herbs and mixed
spice. Mix well, adding more milk or stock if
necessary to make a fairly loose mixture. Season
generously with salt and freshly ground black
pepper and simmer in a little butter until mixture
is partially cooked. Remove from pan and beat
in 2 eggs.

2. To stuff chicken: loosen the skin at the neck
end of a cleaned and trussed roasting chicken as
much as possible from the breast. Insert stuffing
over the flesh of the breast and fill the loose skin of
the neck with as much as it will hold. Fold the skin
over and fasten with 1 or 2 stitches. Stuff the body
cavity as well.

3. To bake chicken: spread coarse sea salt 2.5 cm/ 1 inch thick on the bottom of casserole. Rub chicken lightly with a little softened butter or olive oil and season generously with salt and freshly ground black pepper. Wrap chicken lightly in greaseproof paper and place on bed of sea salt. Pour sea salt around chicken to the top of casserole, mounding salt up to completely cover bird. Place cover on casserole and place in a moderately hot oven (200°C, 400°F, Gas Mark 6) for 1½ hours.

4. To serve: remove casserole cover, break salt crust and remove excess salt from casserole. Lift out chicken, remove greaseproof paper from bird and place chicken on a heated serving platter.

Lemon Grilled Chicken

3 young frying chickens, quartered
salt and freshly ground black pepper

LEMON BARBECUE SAUCE
150 ml/¼ pint olive oil
8 tablespoons lemon juice
4 level tablespoons finely chopped onion
1–2 level teaspoons dried tarragon
1–2 level teaspoons finely chopped parsley
salt and freshly ground black pepper
Tabasco sauce

1. Sprinkle chicken with salt and freshly ground black pepper, and marinate in Lemon Barbecue Sauce for at least 4 hours.

2. When ready to grill, drain chicken pieces and brush with reserved marinade juices. Grill slowly until tender – 45 minutes – turning chicken pieces and basting from time to time.

Grilled Spring Chicken

2 tender poussins (young chickens)
salt and freshly ground black pepper
paprika
lemon juice
melted butter
4 level tablespoons browned breadcrumbs
sprigs of watercress
lemon wedges

Only very young and tender chickens can be cooked in this way.

1. Split cleaned chickens open through the back, flatten and trim birds, cutting off feet and wing-tips. Wipe with a damp cloth, and season generously with salt, freshly ground black pepper, paprika and a little lemon juice. Skewer birds open, brush both sides with melted butter and sprinkle with fine browned breadcrumbs.

2. Grill over charcoal or under grill for 25 to 30 minutes, turning the birds occasionally and basting frequently with melted butter.

3. Serve very hot, garnished with watercress and lemon wedges.

Roast Chicken with Stuffing

1 roasting chicken, cleaned and trussed
stuffing (see choice of stuffings below)
2 rashers fat bacon
butter
sifted flour
watercress
lemon juice
salt
300 ml/½ pint chicken stock
freshly ground black pepper
300 ml/½ pint English Bread Sauce (see
  page 82)

1. Loosen the skin at the neck end of a cleaned and trussed roasting chicken as much as possible from the breast. Insert stuffing over the flesh of the breast and fill the loose skin of the neck with as much as it will hold. Fold the skin over and fasten with 1 or 2 stitches. Stuff body cavity as well.

2. Tie 1 or 2 rashers of fat bacon over the breast, making 1 or 2 slits in the bacon to prevent it from curling. Cover the bird with waxed paper and roast in a moderate oven (160°C, 325°F, Gas Mark 3), basting frequently with butter for 1 to 1½ hours, depending on size and age of the bird. Test it by feeling the flesh of the leg; if it gives way to pressure it is ready.

3. A few minutes before the end of cooking time, remove the paper and bacon and sprinkle the breast lightly with sifted flour. Baste well, and brown quickly.

4. When ready to serve: put bird on a hot serving dish, remove the trussing string, and garnish with watercress seasoned with lemon juice and salt, to taste.

5. Pour off the fat from the roasting tin in which bird was roasted, add chicken stock and stir over a high heat until boiling, scraping in any brown bits from sides of pan. Season to taste with salt and freshly ground black pepper, and serve in a sauceboat.

6. Serve with English Bread Sauce.

Stuffing I: French

liver and heart of bird, finely chopped
1 Spanish onion, finely chopped
2 tablespoons olive oil
2 level tablespoons butter
3 slices white bread, diced
3 level tablespoons finely chopped parsley
salt and freshly ground black pepper
pinch of cayenne
1 egg, beaten
4 tablespoons dry white wine

1. Sauté finely chopped liver, heart and onion in olive oil and butter until golden.

2. Add diced bread and finely chopped parsley and cook for a few minutes, stirring continuously.

3. Season with salt and freshly ground black pepper and cayenne. Transfer mixture to a mixing bowl and allow to cool. Just before stuffing bird, stir in beaten egg and dry white wine.

Stuffing II: Moroccan

½ onion, finely chopped
¼ clove garlic, finely chopped
2 level tablespoons butter
2 level tablespoons olive oil
65 g/2½ oz fresh breadcrumbs
2 level tablespoons finely chopped parsley
4 level tablespoons slivered toasted almonds
4 level tablespoons seedless raisins, soaked
  in hot water
salt and freshly ground black pepper
¼ level teaspoon cumin seed
¼ level teaspoon ground ginger
¼ level teaspoon ground cinnamon
¼ level teaspoon cayenne
1 egg, beaten
4 tablespoons chicken stock

1. Sauté finely chopped onion and garlic in butter and olive oil until the vegetables are soft.

60

2. Add the breadcrumbs and finely chopped parsley and continue to cook, stirring continuously over a low heat, for a few more minutes.

3. Transfer mixture to a mixing bowl and stir in slivered toasted almonds and soaked raisins.

4. Season with salt and freshly ground black pepper, cumin seed, ground ginger, cinnamon and cayenne. Add beaten egg and chicken stock and mix well.

Poulet Sauté 'Quaglino's'

1 tender chicken (1.25–1.5 kg/2½–3 lb)
salt and freshly ground black pepper
4 level tablespoons butter
1 bouquet garni (2 parsley roots, 1 sprig
**   thyme, 1 bay leaf)**
2 level tablespoons finely chopped onion
1 small clove garlic
1 glass dry white wine
450 g/1 lb ripe red tomatoes, peeled, seeded
**   and chopped**
4 button mushrooms, simmered in butter
**   and lemon juice**

1. Cut chicken into serving pieces, reserving backbone. Season well with salt and freshly ground black pepper, and put chicken pieces, flesh side down in a sauté pan or thick-bottomed frying pan just large enough to hold them comfortably. Sauté chicken pieces in butter until they are browned on all sides – about 10 minutes.

2. Add backbone and *bouquet garni*, cover pan and simmer gently for 20 minutes. Remove wings and breasts after 15 minutes. They are the most delicate, and cook most quickly. Keep warm.

3. Remove remaining pieces and sauté finely chopped onion in pan juices until transparent. Add garlic and dry white wine, and continue cooking until wine is reduced to half of the original quantity.

4. Add tomatoes and simmer for 5 minutes more.

5. Return sautéed chicken to the pan, cover and

allow to simmer gently over the lowest of heats for 5 minutes. Do not allow liquid to boil or your chicken will be tough.

6. Garnish with button mushrooms which you have simmered in butter and lemon juice. Serve immediately.

Chicken Stuffed with Grapes
Illustrated on page 86

1 roasting chicken (1.75–2.25 kg/4–5 lb)
butter
salt
freshly ground black pepper
dry white wine

STUFFING
1 Spanish onion, finely chopped
4 cloves garlic, finely chopped
butter
4 slices dry bread, crumbled
100–175 g/4–6 oz white seedless grapes
6 tablespoons melted butter
2 level tablespoons finely chopped parsley
¼ level teaspoon dried sage
salt and freshly ground black pepper

1. To make stuffing: sauté onion and garlic in a little butter and combine with crumbled bread, grapes, melted butter, finely chopped parsley and sage. Season to taste with salt and freshly ground black pepper.

2. Rub chicken on the inside with salt and stuff with the grape stuffing.

3. Skewer the opening. Truss the chicken and rub it with butter, salt and freshly ground black pepper. Roast the bird in a moderate oven (160°C, 325°F, Gas Mark 3) for 1½ to 2 hours, until cooked, basting from time to time with a little dry white wine.

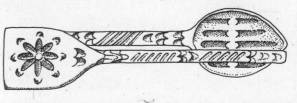

62

Chicken Sauté Alexandra

1 tender chicken (1.25-1.5 kg/2½-3 lb)
salt and freshly ground black pepper
4 level tablespoons butter
1 bouquet garni (2 parsley roots, 1 sprig
   thyme, 1 bay leaf)
150 ml/¼ pint chicken stock
150 ml/¼ pint Chicken Velouté Sauce (see
   page 82)
4 level tablespoons cooked puréed onions
4 level tablespoons double cream

1. Cut chicken into serving pieces, reserving back-bone. Season well with salt and freshly ground black pepper, and put chicken pieces, flesh side down, in a sauté pan or thick-bottomed frying pan just large enough to hold them comfortably. Add 2 tablespoons butter and sauté chicken pieces until they are browned on all sides – about 10 minutes.

2. Add backbone and *bouquet garni*, cover pan and simmer gently for 20 minutes. Remove wings and breasts after 15 minutes. They are the most delicate, and cook most quickly. Keep warm.

3. Remove remaining pieces of chicken, add chicken stock to pan juices and reduce to half of the original quantity.

4. Stir in Chicken Velouté Sauce to which you have added cooked puréed onions, double cream and remaining 2 tablespoons butter. Strain the sauce over chicken pieces and heat through.

Poulet Sauté à la Crème

1 tender chicken (1.25-1.5 kg/2½-3 lb)
salt and freshly ground black pepper
4 level tablespoons butter
1 bouquet garni (2 parsley roots, 1 sprig
   thyme, 1 bay leaf)
300 ml/½ pint double cream

1. Cut chicken into serving pieces, reserving backbone. Season well with salt and freshly ground black pepper, and put chicken pieces, flesh side down, in a sauté pan or thick-bottomed frying pan just large enough to hold them comfortably. Add 2 tablespoons butter and sauté chicken pieces until they are browned on all sides – about 10 minutes.

2. Add backbone and *bouquet garni*, cover pan and simmer gently for 20 minutes. Remove wings and breasts after 15 minutes. They are the most delicate, and cook most quickly. Keep warm.

3. Remove remaining pieces, add cream to pan juices and reduce to half of the original quantity. Stir in remaining 2 tablespoons butter and strain.

4. Add chicken pieces to strained sauce, heat through and serve.

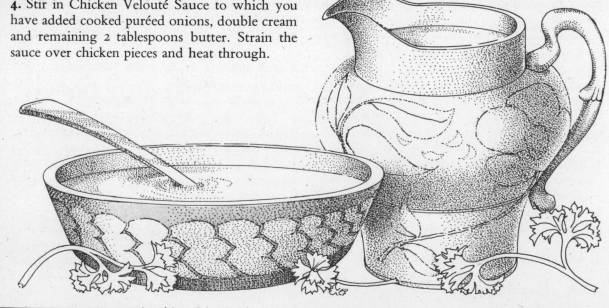

Poulet à la Marengo

1 tender chicken
salt and freshly ground black pepper
2 level tablespoons butter
2 tablespoons olive oil
2 shallots, finely chopped
1 level tablespoon flour
1 glass dry sherry
4 level tablespoons tomato purée
1 bouquet garni (4 sprigs parsley, 1 stick
   celery, 1 bay leaf)
12 button mushrooms, sliced
well-flavoured chicken stock
lemon juice
cayenne
croûtons of fried bread or crescents of
   flaky pastry

1. Cut chicken into serving pieces, removing as much of the skin as possible. Season pieces with salt and freshly ground black pepper, and sauté in butter and olive oil until golden.

2. Sprinkle with finely chopped shallots and flour, and continue to cook, shaking pan, until shallots are transparent. Then add dry sherry, tomato purée, *bouquet garni*, sliced mushrooms and enough well-flavoured stock to cover. Cover and simmer gently in a moderate oven (160°C, 325°F, Gas Mark 3) until chicken is tender.

3. To serve: arrange chicken pieces on a heated serving dish. Skim fat from sauce, add lemon juice and cayenne to taste, and strain sauce over chicken pieces. Garnish with sliced mushrooms and *croûtons* or pastry crescents, and serve immediately.

Poulet Sauté à l'Estragon

63

1 plump chicken
4 tablespoons olive oil
6 level tablespoons finely chopped shallots
1 wine glass very dry white wine
100 ml/4 fl oz water
salt and freshly ground black pepper
450 g/1 lb potatoes, peeled and diced
8 level tablespoons butter
finely chopped fresh tarragon
finely chopped parsley

1. Clean a fine fat chicken and cut it in serving pieces (drumsticks, thighs, wings, and the carcass, cut into 4 or 6 pieces).

2. Sauté chicken pieces in olive oil in a heavy-bottomed ovenproof casserole or iron *cocotte*, turning pieces often until they are evenly golden on all sides.

3. Drain off surplus oil, add finely chopped shallots and stir well, cooking for another minute or two, until shallots are transparent. Add dry white wine and water (the water is to remove the acidity of the wine), and season to taste with salt and freshly ground black pepper. Cover and cook for about 20 minutes, by which time the sauce should be reduced to half of the original quantity. If not, reduce it over a high heat.

4. In the meantime, sauté diced potatoes in 4 tablespoons butter in a frying pan until they are golden.

5. Place chicken pieces on a warm serving dish, add diced cooked potatoes and keep warm.

6. Add finely chopped tarragon and remaining butter to sauce in the casserole. Stir well, taste and correct seasoning. Pour sauce over the diced potatoes and the chicken pieces. Sprinkle with finely chopped parsley.

7. When you serve this dish, mix a little sauce into the potatoes so that they will be well moistened by it. Your sauce should not be too liquid, and there should only be about 2 tablespoons per person.

Chicken with Dumplings

1 large boiling chicken (1.75–2.25 kg/4–5 lb)
1.15 litres/2 pints water
salt
4 carrots
1 Spanish onion stuck with 1 clove
2 sticks celery

SAUCE
3 level tablespoons butter
3 level tablespoons flour
300 ml/½ pint milk

DUMPLINGS
225 g/8 oz self-raising flour, sifted
½ level teaspoon salt
8 level tablespoons melted chicken fat,
 or butter
4 level tablespoons finely chopped parsley
about 150 ml/¼ pint milk

1. To cook chicken: bring water to the boil in a large saucepan. Cut chicken into serving pieces and add to the boiling water with salt and vegetables. Bring to the boil again. Skim, reduce heat and simmer chicken very gently for 3 hours, or until tender. Remove chicken and vegetables from stock. Skim fat from stock, reserving 8 level tablespoons for dumplings. **Note:** if there is not enough chicken fat, make up the amount with melted butter. Strain stock and reserve.

2. To make sauce: melt butter in a small saucepan. Stir in flour until smooth, add milk and cook, stirring constantly until sauce is smooth. Measure 1¼ pints of the chicken stock into a large casserole. Bring to the boil and add cream sauce to stock, stirring constantly. Bring to the boil again and simmer for 5 minutes. Add chicken pieces to sauce.

3. To make dumplings: sift self-raising flour and salt into a mixing bowl. Stir in 8 tablespoons melted chicken fat or butter, and the finely chopped parsley with a fork. Add milk a little at a time, stirring with a fork, or your fingers, until mixture is just dampened. Drop a tablespoonful at a time on to chicken pieces in gently bubbling sauce. Cover and cook for 20 to 25 minutes, until dumplings are cooked through.

Chicken Fricassée

1 tender chicken
juice of 1 lemon
salt
chicken stock
salt and freshly ground black pepper
1 bouquet garni
dry white wine
8 small white onions
2–4 level tablespoons finely chopped parsley
croûtons of bread fried in butter

SAUCE
3 level tablespoons butter
3 level tablespoons flour
8 button mushrooms, sliced
2 egg yolks
double cream (optional)

1. To whiten chicken: clean and wash chicken, cut into serving pieces and put in a saucepan with half the lemon juice and enough cold salted water to cover. Bring to the boil, remove from heat and drain. Plunge into cold water for 5 minutes. Drain.

2. Place chicken in a saucepan with sufficient chicken stock to cover. Add salt, freshly ground black pepper, *bouquet garni*, dry white wine and onions. Bring to the boil, skim and reduce heat; simmer gently until chicken is tender. Remove chicken pieces and onions to a clean casserole and keep warm. Strain and reserve stock for sauce.

3. To make sauce: melt butter in the top of a double saucepan, add flour and stir until smooth. Pour in strained chicken stock and stir over water until boiling. Add sliced mushrooms and simmer gently for 15 minutes. Combine yolks with remaining lemon juice and a little double cream if desired, and stir in a little of the hot sauce. Pour egg and lemon mixture into double saucepan and stir until thick and smooth. Do not allow to boil or sauce will curdle.

4. To serve: place hot cooked chicken pieces and onions in a heated serving bowl. Pour sauce over them and garnish with finely chopped parsley and *croûtons* of fried bread. Serve immediately.

Texas Beef with Oysters (see page 24)

Roast Prime Ribs of Beef (see page 32)

Rare Fillet Stroganoff 'Four Seasons' (see page 29)   Grilled Steak with Roquefort Butter (see page 19)

Old English Beefsteak and Kidney Pie (see page 31)

Chicken Breasts with Foie Gras

breasts of 2 young chickens
4 level tablespoons butter
2 tablespoons olive oil
4 level tablespoons foie gras
450 ml/¾ pint double cream
salt and freshly ground black pepper

1. Separate each half chicken breast into 2 *suprêmes* and sauté them gently in butter and olive oil, covered, until tender but not brown.

2. In the meantime, mix *foie gras* with 4 table-spoons double cream until smooth. Season generously with salt and freshly ground black pepper. Reserve.

3. To finish dish: remove chicken pieces from pan when cooked through. Keep warm. Add remaining cream to pan and bring to the boil. Blend *foie gras* mixture into the sauce and cook, stirring continuously, until smooth. Correct seasoning, pour sauce over chicken pieces and serve immediately.

Twice-Fried Chicken

1 tender chicken (about 1.5 kg/3½ lb)
4 tablespoons soy sauce
8 tablespoons sake or dry sherry diluted
    with a little water
1 level teaspoon sugar
1 level teaspoon fresh root ginger, finely
    chopped
fat or oil for frying
cornflour, sifted

1. Bone chicken and cut the meat into 2.5-cm/1-inch pieces.

2. Combine soy sauce, *sake* (or dry sherry diluted with a little water), sugar and ginger. Marinate chicken pieces in this mixture for at least 2 hours. Drain the chicken thoroughly, reserving marinade juices.

3. Dry the chicken pieces and fry in deep fat until golden. Remove from fat and drain.

4. Add chicken to marinade juices, stirring well so that all pieces are coated by marinade. Allow to stand in marinade for at least 15 minutes. Drain the chicken pieces.

5. Dust lightly with sifted cornflour and fry again in deep fat until crisp and golden brown.

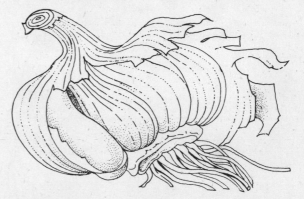

Fried Chicken Strips

450 g/1 lb raw chicken breast
1 egg, beaten
2 tablespoons finely chopped onion
1 clove garlic, finely chopped
2 level tablespoons cornflour
1 tablespoon soy sauce
1 tablespoon sake
2 level teaspoons sugar
salt
fat for deep-frying
finely chopped parsley

1. Remove skin from chicken breast and slice across grain into strips, 5 mm/1¼ inches wide.

2. Place chicken strips in a bowl; add beaten egg, and finely chopped onion and garlic. Sprinkle with cornflour, soy sauce, *sake*, sugar, and salt, to taste. Mix well. Marinate chicken strips in this mixture for 10 to 15 minutes.

3. Fry strips, one at a time, in deep hot fat until golden. Drain.

4. Just before serving, fry again. Garnish with finely chopped parsley and serve immediately.
Serves 4 in a Chinese meal or 2 as a main course on its own.

69

70

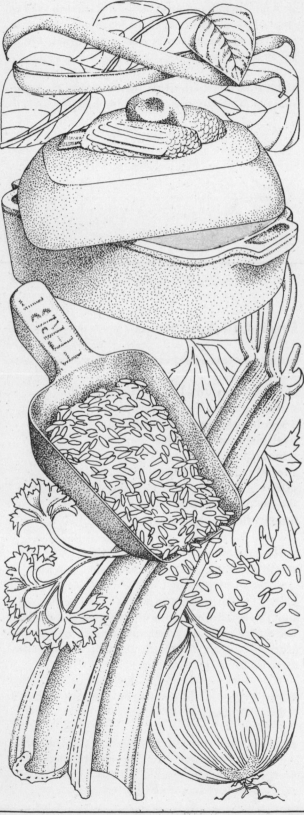

Boiled Chicken with Rice
Illustrated on page 85

1 fat chicken
1 Spanish onion, stuck with 2 cloves
2 large carrots
1 bouquet garni (celery leaves, 2 sprigs
    parsley, 2 sprigs thyme)
2 sticks celery
1 glass dry white wine
1.15 litres/2 pints white stock (chicken or
    veal, or both)
salt and black peppercorns

RICE
1 tablespoon butter
1 Spanish onion, finely chopped
225 g/8 oz rice
300 ml/½ pint strained chicken stock
600 ml/1 pint hot water
salt and freshly ground black pepper

CREAM SAUCE
2 tablespoons flour
2 tablespoons butter
150 ml/¼ pint strained chicken stock
450 ml/¾ pint double cream
salt and freshly ground black pepper
freshly grated nutmeg

GARNISH
cooked carrots
cooked green beans

1. Clean, singe and truss chicken; place in a casserole with an onion stuck with cloves. Add carrots, *bouquet garni* and celery, and moisten with dry white wine and a good white stock. Season to taste with salt and a few peppercorns and simmer gently for about 1½ hours, or until tender.

2. Remove chicken and keep warm. Strain chicken stock, and use for cooking rice and for cream sauce.

3. To prepare rice: Melt butter in a saucepan, add finely chopped onion and stir for a minute over heat until transparent. Stir in rice. Add 300 ml/½ pint strained chicken stock and hot water; season to taste with salt and black pepper. Simmer very gently, covered, for about 25 minutes, or until tender but not mushy.

4. To make cream sauce: Make a white *roux* with flour and butter; add 150 ml/¼ pint chicken stock and double cream, and bring slowly to the boil, stirring constantly. Simmer, stirring from time to time, until sauce is thick and smooth. Remove from heat. Season to taste with salt, black pepper and nutmeg.

5. To serve: Place boiled chicken in the centre of a large heated serving platter. Surround with colourful clusters of cooked whole carrots, green beans and rice. Pour a little cream sauce over chicken and serve the rest separately.

Spanish Fried Chicken

4 chicken breasts
2 leeks (white parts only), finely chopped
4 sprigs parsley
1 bay leaf
150 ml/¼ pint dry white wine
150 ml/¼ pint chicken stock
salt and freshly ground black pepper
300 ml/½ pint Béchamel Sauce (see page 90)
flour
2 eggs, well beaten
fine breadcrumbs
oil for frying

SPINACH PURÉE
1 kg/2 lb spinach
4 tablespoons butter
4 tablespoons chicken stock
freshly ground black pepper
Béchamel Sauce (see page 90)
2 egg yolks, well beaten
salt

1. Place chicken breasts in a well-buttered shallow *gratin* dish with finely chopped leeks, parsley, bay leaf, equal parts dry white wine and chicken stock, salt and freshly ground black pepper, to taste. Cover with a piece of well-buttered foil and poach in a moderately hot oven (200°C, 400°F, Gas Mark 6) until tender. Allow chicken to cool in dish in which it was cooked, then drain.

2. Coat each breast with well-flavoured Béchamel Sauce and allow to cool on a wire rack until sauce is firm.

3. Dip each breast in flour, then in beaten egg, and then toss in fine breadcrumbs, pressing breadcrumbs well against chicken breast with a spatula.

4. To make spinach purée: wash spinach several times in cold water. Combine in a large saucepan with butter, chicken stock, and freshly ground black pepper, to taste. Cook over a high heat, stirring constantly, until spinach is tender – about 5 minutes. Drain and squeeze dry, chop and then purée in electric blender. Combine spinach with a little Béchamel Sauce and beaten egg yolks. Correct seasoning and reheat in the top of a double saucepan until ready to use.

5. Just before serving, fry chicken breasts in deep hot oil until golden. Serve on bed of puréed spinach.

Japanese Chicken

1 tender chicken (about 1.5 kg/3½ lb)
2-4 tablespoons soy sauce
4-6 tablespoons sake or dry sherry diluted
   with a little water
1 level tablespoon brown sugar
15 g/½ oz root ginger, finely chopped
2 shallots, finely chopped
4 slices lemon, coarsely chopped
1 clove garlic, coarsely chopped
cornflour
4 tablespoons peanut or olive oil

1. Combine soy sauce, *sake* (or sherry and water), sugar, chopped root ginger, shallots, lemon and garlic.

2. Cut chicken into serving pieces and dust with a little cornflour. Marinate in mixture for at least 4 hours, turning chicken in juices from time to time.

3. Place chicken in a shallow baking dish and sprinkle with peanut or olive oil. Bake in a moderate oven (160°C, 325°F, Gas Mark 3) for 1 to 1½ hours, basting from time to time.

Turkey with Orange Sauce

72

1 medium-sized turkey (about 4.5 kg/10 lb)
1 orange
1 Spanish onion
2 tablespoons olive oil
salt and freshly ground black pepper
¼ level teaspoon dried rosemary
¼ level teaspoon dried oregano
100 g/4 oz butter, melted
4-6 rashers unsmoked bacon
150 ml/¼ pint dry white wine
juice of 2 oranges
1 clove garlic, finely chopped
1 chicken stock cube

ORANGE SAUCE
turkey giblets
1 Spanish onion, coarsely chopped
1 bay leaf
4 sprigs celery leaves
4 sprigs parsley
salt and freshly ground black pepper
150 ml/¼ pint dry white wine
2 tablespoons butter
2 tablespoons flour
stock from giblets
pan juices

1. Dice unpeeled orange; peel and dice onion. Toss in a mixing bowl with olive oil, salt, freshly ground black pepper, rosemary and oregano.

2. Stuff bird loosely with this mixture. Brush bird with a little melted butter and season generously with salt and freshly ground black pepper. Place in a roasting tin, breast side up. Cover breast with bacon slices and roast bird in a moderate oven (160°C, 325°F, Gas Mark 3) for 30 minutes. Baste turkey with basting sauce made of remaining melted butter, dry white wine and orange juice, seasoned with finely chopped garlic, chicken stock cube, salt and freshly ground black pepper, to taste. Cover loosely with foil and continue to cook for 3 to 4 hours, basting frequently, until turkey is tender. Remove and discard orange and onion stuffing before serving.

3. To make Orange Sauce: wash giblets, and combine neck, heart and gizzard in a saucepan with coarsely chopped onion, bay leaf, celery leaves, parsley, salt and freshly ground black pepper, dry white wine and enough water to cover. Bring to the boil, skim, lower heat and simmer for 1½ hours, adding more water from time to time. Add liver and continue cooking for 30 minutes more. Remove heart, gizzard and liver, and chop pieces coarsely. Melt butter in the top of a double saucepan. Add flour and stir until smooth. Add strained stock from giblets and pan juices (with fat removed), and cook over water, stirring constantly, until sauce is smooth and thick. Add chopped giblets and heat through; correct seasoning and serve with turkey.

Roast Duckling Farci à la Grecque

1 Aylesbury duckling (about 2.25 kg/5 lb)
175 g/6 oz bourgourie (Greek ground wheat)
well-flavoured chicken stock
1 Spanish onion, unpeeled
duck's liver, heart and gizzard
butter
4 level tablespoons finely chopped shallots
  or onion
2 level tablespoons dried currants
4-6 level tablespoons blanched almonds,
  chopped
grated rind of 1 orange
sage
salt and freshly ground black pepper
flour
dry white wine
orange juice

1. Simmer *bourgourie* in chicken stock with 1 unpeeled Spanish onion until tender, then drain. Remove onion, peel and chop finely.

2. Chop liver, heart and gizzard, and sauté in butter with finely chopped shallots. Soak currants in a little hot water until soft. Drain.

3. Combine *bourgourie*, chopped onion, giblets, currants and chopped almonds in a bowl, and mix well. Add grated orange rind and rubbed sage, salt and freshly ground black pepper, to taste. Then add 4 tablespoons melted butter and mix well.

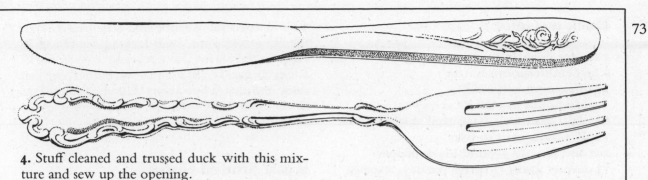

73

4. Stuff cleaned and trussed duck with this mixture and sew up the opening.

5. Place duck, breast side up on a rack in a roasting tin. Cover breast of the bird with buttered foil and roast in a moderate oven (180°C, 350°F, Gas Mark 4) for 1½ to 1¾ hours. Baste frequently with butter or dripping. Remove foil 20 minutes before removing duck from the oven. Dredge breast with flour and leave in oven until well browned. Transfer to a hot serving dish, remove trussing threads and strings. Skim fat from pan juices in roasting tin, stir in a little dry white wine and orange juice. Bring to the boil on top of the cooker, stirring in all crusty bits from sides and bottom of pan. Reduce heat and simmer for 2 to 3 minutes. Strain into sauceboat and serve with duck.

Caneton de Colette

1 plump duck (about 2.25 kg/5 lb)
1-2 duck livers
butter
salt and freshly ground black pepper
allspice
½ glass cognac
½ glass port
stock (optional)

1. Clean, singe and truss a plump duck. Remove wishbone to help carving, and roast duck in a moderately hot oven (200°C, 400°F, Gas Mark 6) for 25 minutes, or until flesh is pink when cut.

2. Sauté duck livers in butter for a minute or two until they stiffen but are not cooked through. Add pan juices from duck, then mash livers with a fork and season generously with salt, freshly ground black pepper and allspice. Pour warmed cognac and port over sauce, ignite and reduce over a high heat to three-quarters of the original quantity.

3. Remove drumsticks and wings from duck, and sauté in butter until cooked through.

4. Remove breast of duck, cut into long fine strips and sauté in butter. Arrange in centre of heated serving dish.

5. Cut carcass in half and press in a duck press to obtain as much blood and juices as possible (or cut duck carcass into 4 to 6 pieces and press each piece with pincers to obtain juices). Mix these juices with mashed livers, adding a little stock if necessary, and heat through until bubbling.

6. Arrange drumsticks and wings on serving dish. Correct seasoning of sauce and strain through a fine sieve over strips of meat and drumsticks.

Devilled Duck, Chicken or Turkey

6 portions cold roast duck, chicken or turkey
100 g/4 oz softened butter
1 level tablespoon Dijon mustard
1 level teaspoon English mustard
2 level tablespoons chutney
1 level teaspoon curry powder
1-2 tablespoons lemon juice
salt
cayenne

1. Score poultry with a sharp knife.

2. Combine butter, mustards, chutney, curry powder and lemon juice in a mortar, and pound to a smooth paste. Season to taste with salt and cayenne.

3. Spread mixture on cold duck, chicken or turkey, and grill until sizzling hot.

74

Duck en Gelée

1 tender duckling
6 level tablespoons butter
2 tablespoons olive oil
8 tablespoons dry white wine
600 ml/1 pint well-flavoured chicken stock
1 calf's foot, split in two
salt and freshly ground black pepper
1 bouquet garni (2 sprigs parsley, 2 sprigs
   thyme, 1 stick celery, 2 bay leaves)
12 cubes fat bacon
12 young turnips
12 button mushrooms
12 button onions
100 g/4 oz lean beef, minced
whites and shells of 2 eggs
2 level tablespoons gelatine
green salad

1. Clean duckling, cut into serving pieces. Sauté in 4 level tablespoons butter and 2 tablespoons olive oil in a flameproof casserole until golden on all sides. Moisten with dry white wine and bring to the boil. Add chicken stock, calf's foot, salt, freshly ground black pepper and a *bouquet garni*. Reduce heat and simmer gently for 30 minutes, skimming from time to time.

2. Sauté bacon cubes in remaining butter until golden. Remove, and sauté turnips in resulting fat until golden.

3. Combine sautéed bacon and turnips with button mushrooms and onions, and add to duckling. Cover and simmer for about 1½ hours, or until duckling is tender and vegetables are cooked through, basting duckling from time to time.

4. Remove duckling to an oval *terrine* just large enough to hold it, and surround with bacon cubes, turnips, mushrooms and onions.

5. To clarify stock: strain stock into a clean saucepan; add minced beef and the whites and shells of 2 eggs and bring gradually to the boil over a low heat, stirring frequently. Stop stirring when thick pad of foam forms on top of liquid. Simmer for 30 minutes. Whilst hot, strain stock through a sieve lined with a wet flannel cloth.

6. Soften gelatine in a little cold water and stir into the hot stock. Pour over duckling, covering it. **Note:** if there is not enough liquid to cover duckling completely, add equal quantities chicken stock and dry white wine. Allow to set for 12 hours before unmoulding. Serve with a green salad.

Roast Stuffed Goose

1 fat goose (3.5-4.5 kg/8-10 lb)
melted butter
salt and freshly ground black pepper
4-6 tablespoons Calvados or cognac
dried breadcrumbs

STUFFING
1 Spanish onion, finely chopped
4 level tablespoons butter
2 tablespoons olive oil
225 g/8 oz sausagemeat
4 level tablespoons finely chopped parsley
2 eggs, well beaten
juice of ½ lemon
crushed dried thyme and sage
salt and freshly ground black pepper
50-75 g/2-3 oz dried breadcrumbs

Note: If goose is frozen, leave in the original wrappings and thaw for 48 hours in the refrigerator. Remove wrapping and drain liquids from cavity of goose.

Or, remove wrappings from frozen goose and thaw overnight in a container of water. Drain.

Then chop off tips of wings. Cut all excess fat from cavity and reserve for frying potatoes or some other use. Remove giblets and save for goose stock or sauce.

The gizzard, heart and liver are also good braised with goose fat and finely chopped onion and sliced thinly to be served with salad greens (young lettuce and spinach leaves, *mache* and curly endive) as an appetiser salad.

1. To make stuffing: sauté finely chopped onion in butter and olive oil until transparent. Add

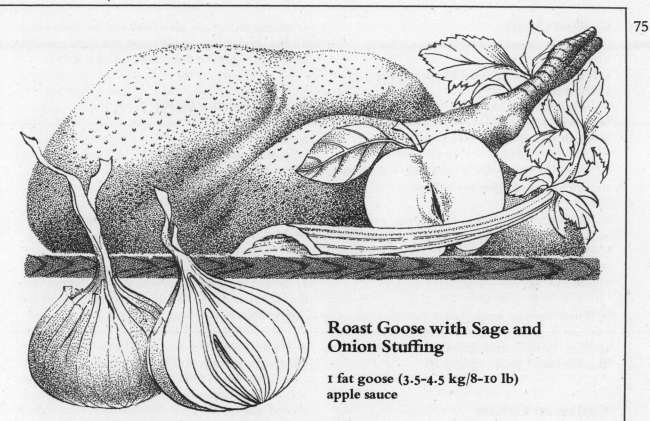

Roast Goose with Sage and Onion Stuffing

I fat goose (3.5–4.5 kg/8–10 lb)
apple sauce

sausagemeat and sauté with onion until golden. Combine onion and sausage mixture in a bowl with finely chopped parsley. Stir in eggs, lemon juice, thyme, sage, salt and freshly ground black pepper, to taste. Add breadcrumbs and mix well.

2. Stuff and tie goose, brush lightly with melted butter and season generously with salt and freshly ground black pepper. Roast in a moderately hot oven (200°C, 400°F, Gas Mark 6) for 15 minutes. Reduce heat to moderate (150°C, 300°F, Gas Mark 2) and continue roasting until goose is tender – about 25 minutes per half kilo/per lb.

3. Skim off fat several times during cooking and baste goose with pan juices. The reserved fat will keep indefinitely in a cool place.

4. If you cover goose with foil, remove foil at least 45 minutes before end of cooking time. Flame goose with heated Calvados or cognac 15 minutes before the end of cooking time, then sprinkle lightly with dried breadcrumbs. Raise oven heat to hot (230°C, 450°F, Gas Mark 8) and cook for 15 minutes.

STUFFING
225 g/8 oz butter
450 g/1 lb Spanish onions, chopped
175 g/6 oz celery, chopped
1 small loaf, freshly grated
2 eggs, well beaten
1 large cooking apple, peeled, cored and diced
1 level tablespoon powdered sage
salt
freshly ground black pepper

See Note for Roast Stuffed Goose.

I. To make stuffing: melt butter, and sauté onions and celery until golden. Combine with breadcrumbs, beaten eggs, diced apple, sage, salt and freshly ground black pepper, to taste.

2. Lightly stuff the goose. Truss and place on a rack in a shallow roasting tin. Roast in a cool oven (150°C, 300°F, Gas Mark 2) for about 25 minutes per half kilo/per lb. Prick the skin occasionally to let the fat run out. Skim fat from roasting tin from time to time. Serve goose with apple sauce.

76

Grilled Quail

8 quail
salt and freshly ground black pepper
melted butter
8 croûtons fried bread
watercress
English Bread Sauce (see page 82)

1. Split quail through the backbone and lay them flat without separating the halves.

2. Wipe them carefully and season generously with salt and freshly ground black pepper. Brush with butter and grill for 5 to 6 minutes on one side. Turn birds; brush with butter and grill for 5 to 6 minutes on the other side, until tender.

3. When quail are ready to be served, place each bird on a *croûton* of bread fried in butter until golden; garnish with sprigs of watercress. Serve English Bread Sauce separately.

Cailles en Caisses

4-8 quail, according to size
1 (60-g/2⅜-oz) can mousse de foie gras
truffles
2 level tablespoons butter
1 tablespoon olive oil
2 small carrots, diced
1 medium-sized onion, diced
salt and freshly ground black pepper
well-flavoured stock (optional)
Brown Chaudfroid Sauce (see page 83)
chopped Aspic Jelly (see page 83)

1. Bone quail and stuff them with *mousse de foie gras*, putting a truffle or part of a truffle in the centre of each. Sew them up, making them as neat a shape as possible.

2. Braise birds in butter and olive oil with diced carrots and onion for 15 to 20 minutes or poach them in a little well-flavoured stock with diced carrot and onion until tender. Season with salt and freshly ground black pepper. Remove pan from heat and cool. Remove trussing threads and coat each quail with Brown Chaudfroid Sauce.

3. When set, place each bird in an individual shallow ramekin or soufflé dish just large enough to hold it. Garnish with chopped aspic jelly.

Roast Guinea Fowl

2 guinea fowl
½ Spanish onion, halved
½ lemon, halved
6 juniper berries, crushed
½ level teaspoon dried thyme
salt and freshly ground black pepper
melted butter
watercress

1. Divide the onion, lemon, juniper berries and thyme between the two birds and use to stuff the cavity in each.

2. Skewer openings and truss birds. Season with salt and freshly ground black pepper, and roast in a moderate oven (160°C, 325°F, Gas Mark 3) for 50 to 60 minutes, until tender, basting birds with melted butter every 10 minutes. Serve garnished with sprigs of watercress.

Herbed Guinea Fowl

2 guinea fowl
2 cloves garlic, finely chopped
½ level teaspoon dried thyme
6 level tablespoons softened butter
grated peel of ¼ lemon
lemon juice
salt and freshly ground black pepper

1. Cut guinea fowl into quarters.

2. Pound garlic, thyme, butter and lemon peel to a smooth paste with lemon juice, salt and freshly ground black pepper, to taste.

3. Rub birds with this mixture and place in a well-buttered *gratin* dish. Cook in a moderately hot oven (190°C, 375°F, Gas Mark 5) for 40 to 50 minutes, until tender.

4. Cool; wrap loosely in foil until ready to use.

Roast Grouse with Juniper Berries

4 young grouse (225–450 g/½–1 lb each)
4 level tablespoons softened butter
8–12 juniper berries, crushed
juice of 1 lemon
salt and freshly ground black pepper
8 thin rashers bacon
4 croûtons big enough to serve as base for
   grouse
clarified butter
1 tablespoon olive oil
1–2 tablespoons cognac
watercress
redcurrant jelly

1. Combine softened butter, crushed juniper berries and lemon juice in a mixing bowl; add salt and a generous amount of freshly ground black pepper, to taste.

2. Rub birds inside and out with this mixture. Tie 2 thin rashers of fat bacon over the breast of each bird and roast in a hot oven (220°C, 425°F, Gas Mark 7) for 20 to 25 minutes.

3. When birds are half cooked, remove livers and mash them slightly. Place in roasting tin to cook with grouse until birds are tender. Skim fat from tin.

4. Just before serving, fry *croûtons* in a little clarified butter and olive oil until golden. Spread with mashed livers and crusty bits from roasting tin which you have seasoned to taste with cognac, salt and freshly ground black pepper, to taste.

5. To serve: remove bacon and string, place each bird on a garnished *croûton* and arrange on a heated serving dish. Serve with watercress and redcurrant jelly.

Spatchcocked Grouse

4 young grouse (225–450 g/½–1 lb each)
salt and freshly ground black pepper
2 level tablespoons finely chopped parsley
2 level tablespoons finely chopped shallots
   (optional)
melted butter
dried thyme or crushed juniper berries
Maître d'Hôtel Butter (see below)
game potato chips or grilled mushrooms

Only very young and tender birds can be prepared in this way.

1. Split them through the back without separating the halves, wipe the pieces carefully with a damp cloth and skewer them open. Season generously with salt, freshly ground black pepper and finely chopped parsley and shallots (optional). Brush birds with melted butter and season with a little dried thyme or crushed juniper berries.

2. Grease grid and make it very hot. Place birds on it and grill them over a high heat, turning them occasionally and brushing them with more butter when necessary. Cooking time will depend very much on the size and thickness of the grouse.

3. When cooked to your liking (grouse should never be overcooked), place the birds on a very hot dish with a pat of Maître d'Hôtel Butter on the top of each one. Garnish with game potato chips or grilled mushrooms.

Maître d'Hôtel Butter

100 g/4 oz butter
1 tablespoon finely chopped parsley
1 tablespoon lemon juice
salt and freshly ground black pepper

Cream butter with finely chopped parsley and lemon juice. Season to taste with salt and freshly ground black pepper. Chill.

Game Pie

78

2 partridges or pheasants
350 g/12 oz veal cutlets
225 g/8 oz cooked ham
6 tablespoons cognac
6 tablespoons red wine
2 level tablespoons finely chopped parsley
4 level tablespoons finely chopped onion
salt and freshly ground black pepper
butter
3 tablespoons olive oil
100 g/4 oz button mushrooms, quartered
$\frac{1}{4}$ level teaspoon dried thyme
1 bay leaf
300 ml/$\frac{1}{2}$ pint well-flavoured game stock
Puff Pastry (see page 91)
1 egg yolk

1. Cut partridges (or pheasants) into serving pieces, removing bones where possible.

2. Cut veal and ham into 1-cm/$\frac{1}{2}$-inch strips.

3. Marinate meats in cognac and red wine for at least 4 hours, with finely chopped parsley, onion, salt and freshly ground black pepper, to taste.

4. Preheat oven to hot (230°C, 450°F, Gas Mark 8).

5. Line a deep pie dish with strips of ham and veal. Sauté partridge or pheasant pieces in 3 tablespoons each butter and olive oil until golden, then place them on this bed. Top with quartered mushrooms, and season generously with salt, freshly ground black pepper, dried thyme and a bay leaf. Pour over marinade juices and game stock, and dot with 2 tablespoons diced butter.

6. Cover pie dish with a double thickness of aluminium foil; place in preheated oven and cook for 20 minutes. Reduce heat to moderate (180°C, 350°F, Gas Mark 4) and continue to cook for 45 minutes, or until meats are tender. Remove from oven and cool.

7. Line the rims of the pie dish with strips of puff pastry, and then cover pie with remaining pastry. Make a hole in the centre and decorate with pastry leaves. Brush with egg yolk and cook in a hot oven (230°C, 450°F, Gas Mark 8) for 10 minutes, or until pastry begins to brown, then reduce heat to moderate (180°C, 350°F, Gas Mark 4) and continue cooking for 20 to 30 minutes, until the pastry is brown and crisp.

Roast Wild Duck

2 wild ducks
salt and freshly ground black pepper
dried thyme
2 oranges
2 tart apples
2 Spanish onions
8 rashers bacon
300 ml/$\frac{1}{2}$ pint port

GARNISH
orange slices
watercress

SAUCE
2 level tablespoons flour
juice of 1 orange
juice of 1 lemon
port
salt and freshly ground black pepper

1. Clean, pluck and singe wild ducks. Rub cavities with salt, freshly ground black pepper and dried thyme.

2. Chop unpeeled oranges, apples and onions coarsely, and stuff ducks loosely with this flavouring mixture, keeping any remaining mixture for placing around ducks in roasting tins. Place ducks, breast sides up, on rack in roasting tins, cover the breasts with bacon and pour port into the tins.

3. Roast ducks in a hot oven (230°C, 450°F, Gas Mark 8) for 20 minutes, basting several times with port.

4. Remove bacon, baste well with pan juices and continue roasting for 10 to 15 more minutes until ducks are tender but rare. Crisp skins under grill, then transfer ducks to a heated serving dish and keep warm.

5. To make sauce: skim most of fat from pan juices, and stir in flour which you have dissolved in orange and lemon juice. Stir over a high heat, incorporating all crusty bits, until sauce thickens. Then add port, salt and freshly ground black pepper, to taste.

6. To serve: garnish ducks with orange slices and fresh watercress. Serve.

Roast Pheasant

2 tender pheasants (about 1.25 kg/2½ lb each)
salt and freshly ground black pepper
2 slices fat salt pork or fat bacon
chicken stock
red wine
watercress
English Bread Sauce (see page 82) or browned breadcrumbs

STUFFING
1 cooking apple
4 tablespoons soften
juice of ½ lemon
4 tablespoons finely chop   nion
2 tablespoons olive oil
salt and freshly ground   pper

GRAVY
150 ml/¼ pint chicken stock
2 tablespoons redcurrant jelly
2 tablespoons fresh breadcrumbs

1. To make stuffing: grate apple coarsely and combine with softened butter, lemon juice and finely chopped onion which you have softened in olive oil. Season generously with salt and freshly ground black pepper.

2. Stuff birds with this mixture. Season with salt and freshly ground black pepper. Tie a thin slice of fat salt pork or bacon over the breasts and roast in a moderate oven (180°C, 350°F, Gas Mark 4) for about 1 hour, or until tender, basting from time to time with chicken stock and red wine.

3. To make gravy: skim fat from pan juices and combine 150 ml/¼ pint of the pan juices

(made up, if necessary with water and red wine), with stock, redcurrant jelly and breadcrumbs. Simmer gently, stirring, until thickened.

4. To serve: remove bacon and strings and transfer birds to a heated serving dish. Garnish with watercress and serve with gravy and English Bread Sauce or browned breadcrumbs.

Pheasant Mousse

175 g/6 oz pheasant breast, cooked
50 g/2 oz ham
150 ml/¼ pint extra thick White Sauce (see page 84)
2 eggs
4 level tablespoons softened butter
1-2 tablespoons dry sherry
salt and freshly ground black pepper
pinch of nutmeg
grated lemon rind
150 ml/¼ pint double cream, stiffly whipped
clarified butter
a few cooked green peas, or finely chopped parsley and truffles
French Tomato Sauce (see page 90)

1. Mince pheasant with ham, and pound until smooth in a mortar with Extra-thick White Sauce, 2 eggs and softened butter.

2. Rub mixture through a fine sieve into a bowl. Add sherry, salt, freshly ground black pepper, nutmeg and grated lemon rind. Mix well, then fold in stiffly whipped cream.

3. Grease a plain mould with clarified butter and decorate with cooked green peas, or finely chopped parsley an_   _es cut in fancy shapes. Pour in the pheasa_   e and cover with greased greaseproof pa_   ace mould in a pan two-thirds full of boiling water and cook in a moderate oven (180°C, 350°F, Gas Mark 4) until mousse is firm to the touch.

4. Allow mousse to stand for a few minutes after removing it from the oven. Turn out carefully on to a serving dish and pour French Tomato Sauce around it.

79

80

Grilled Venison Steaks

**4 venison steaks
salt and freshly ground black pepper
2 bay leaves, crumbled
4 tablespoons olive oil
2 tablespoons lemon juice
6 level tablespoons softened butter
red or blackcurrant jelly**

1. Choose the steaks from the leg if possible, cut from 1.5-2.5 cm/¾-1 inch in thickness. Trim them neatly and season with salt, freshly ground black pepper and crumbled bay leaves. Marinate them in olive oil and lemon juice for 2 hours.

2. Drain and grill as you would beef, turning them often and allowing rather longer than for a beef steak. Venison must be served immediately, or it will become tough.

3. To serve: transfer steaks on to a heated serving dish and garnish with softened butter to which you have added red or blackcurrant jelly, to taste.

Marinated Venison Steaks

**4 thick steaks of venison, cut from the loin
salt and freshly ground black pepper
½ Spanish onion, sliced
2 carrots, sliced
4 sprigs parsley
2 bay leaves
thyme and rosemary
150 ml/¼ pint dry white wine
8 tablespoons olive oil
2 tablespoons butter**

SAUCE
**2 tablespoons butter
2 shallots, finely chopped
1 tablespoon flour
6 tablespoons marinade juices, strained
200 ml/7 fl oz soured cream
lemon juice
freshly ground black pepper**

1. Season venison steaks generously with salt and freshly ground black pepper, and combine in a

bowl with sliced onion and carrots, parsley, bay leaves, thyme and rosemary. Moisten with dry white wine and 6 tablespoons olive oil. Place bowl in the refrigerator and marinate steaks for 24 to 48 hours, turning them occasionally.

2. To cook steaks: remove venison from marinade, reserving marinade juices for further use, and pat dry. Heat 2 tablespoons each olive oil and butter in a large thick-bottomed frying pan, and sauté venison over a high heat for about 3 minutes on each side. Remove and keep warm.

3. To make sauce: drain excess fat from frying pan, add 2 tablespoons butter and sauté finely chopped shallots until soft. Sprinkle with flour and cook, stirring, until the *roux* is lightly browned. Add 6 tablespoons strained marinade juices, the soured cream, lemon juice and freshly ground black pepper, to taste.

4. Serve steaks on a heated serving dish with sauce.

Woodcock au Fumet

**2 woodcock
2 rashers bacon
salt and freshly ground black pepper
olive oil
2 shallots, finely chopped, or ¼ Spanish onion, finely chopped
300 ml/½ pint champagne
300 ml/½ pint port
2 level tablespoons tomato purée
2 slices white bread
butter
4 level tablespoons sieved pâté de foie gras
2 tablespoons cognac**

1. Hang woodcock for 4 to 6 days.

2. Clean and draw birds, reserving the livers. Truss legs close to the body and tie a rasher of bacon around each bird. Season generously with salt and freshly ground black pepper, and roast in a hot oven (220°C, 425°F, Gas Mark 7) for 10 to 15 minutes. Cut threads and discard bacon. Cut 2 *suprêmes* (breast and wings) and legs from birds, and reserve.

3. Chop carcasses finely and put them in a saucepan with a little olive oil and finely chopped shallots, or onion. Simmer until shallots are soft. Add champagne, port and tomato purée, and continue cooking for a few minutes.

4. Chop the raw livers and add them, together with the juices in the roasting tin in which the birds were cooked, to the chopped carcasses; simmer sauce for 30 minutes.

5. Cut bread slices in half, trim crusts and sauté slices in butter until golden. Spread with sieved *foie gras*. Place them on a heated serving dish.

6. Warm woodcock *suprêmes* and legs through in a little butter, sprinkle with cognac and flame.

7. To serve: arrange woodcock pieces on *canapés* and rub sauce over birds through a fine sieve. Serve immediately.

Partridge en Salade

2 partridges
150 ml/¼ pint olive oil
4 level tablespoons finely chopped shallots or onion
wine vinegar
4 level tablespoons finely chopped chervil or parsley
salt and freshly ground black pepper
dry mustard
2 apples, peeled and diced
2 sticks celery, sliced

1. Roast partridges in a moderately hot oven (200°C, 400°F, Gas Mark 6) for 18 to 20 minutes. Cut into serving pieces. Slice breasts.

2. Combine partridge pieces in a bowl with olive oil and finely chopped shallots, or onion. Marinate in this mixture for at least 12 hours, turning pieces from time to time.

3. When ready to serve, remove partridges from marinade and arrange them in a serving bowl. Make a well-flavoured *vinaigrette* with the oil in the dish by adding wine vinegar, finely chopped

chervil or parsley, salt, freshly ground black pepper and dry mustard, to taste. Pour *vinaigrette* mixture over partridges and add diced apples and celery. Toss and serve.

Lièvre à la Broche 'Paul Bocuse'

1 young hare (about 2 kg/4½ lb)
salt and freshly ground black pepper
powdered thyme and rosemary
Dijon mustard
olive oil
Rice Pilaff (see page 13)

SAUCE
2 shallots, finely chopped
pan juices
2 tablespoons wine vinegar
450 ml/¾ pint soured cream
2 juniper berries, crushed

1. Do not marinate hare. Rub it with a damp cloth and put it on a spit. Season the hare inside and out with salt, freshly ground black pepper, powdered thyme and rosemary, to taste, then coat it generously with Dijon mustard. Sprinkle with a little olive oil and roast it on the spit for 35 to 40 minutes, or until the hare is tender but the flesh is still rose-coloured. Make sure there is a pan under the hare to catch the juices as it cooks.

2. To make sauce: simmer finely chopped shallots in pan juices until soft. Add wine vinegar and scrape all the crusty bits from the sides of the pan. Then add soured cream and crushed juniper berries, and reduce the sauce to one-third of the original quantity. Strain.

3. Serve the hare with sauce and a Rice Pilaff.

Sauces

82

Basic Meat Aspic

225 g/8 oz beef bones
duck or chicken carcass, if available
1 calf's foot or 4 cleaned chicken feet
1 Spanish onion, sliced
1 large leek, sliced
2 large carrots, sliced
2 sticks celery, chopped
1.15 litres/2 pints water
salt and freshly ground black pepper
1 bouquet garni (parsley, 1 sprig thyme,
  1 bay leaf)
1 egg white
100 g/4 oz raw lean beef, chopped
1 teaspoon finely chopped chervil and
  tarragon

1. Combine first ten ingredients in a large stock-pot, bring slowly to the boil and simmer gently for about 4 hours, removing scum from time to time. Strain and cool before skimming off the fat.

2. **To clarify stock:** beat egg white lightly, and combine with chopped lean beef and herbs in the bottom of a large saucepan. Add the cooled stock and mix well, bring stock to the boil, stirring constantly. Lower heat and simmer the stock very gently for about 15 minutes. Strain through a flannel cloth while still hot. Allow to cool and then stir in one of the following:

Sherry Aspic
Stir in 4 tablespoons dry sherry.

Madeira Aspic
Stir in 4 tablespoons Madeira.

Port Aspic
Stir in 4 tablespoons port wine.

Tarragon Aspic
When clarifying aspic, add 6 additional sprigs of tarragon.

This recipe will make 1.15 litres/2 pints of jelly and will keep for several days in the refrigerator.

Basic Game Aspic
Prepare game aspic in the same way as basic meat aspic. Reinforce its flavour with 100 g/4 oz lean chopped beef and 100 g/4 oz lean dark meat from the particular game the aspic is to be served with – partridge, pheasant, grouse, etc. – when you add egg white and fresh herbs to clarify the stock. I always add a tablespoon or two of *fine champagne* to game aspic after it has been clarified to improve the flavour further.

English Bread Sauce

300 ml/½ pint milk
½ onion stuck with 1–2 cloves
50 g/2 oz fresh breadcrumbs
2–3 tablespoons butter or double cream
salt and white pepper
pinch of cayenne

1. Simmer milk and onion stuck with cloves until the milk is well flavoured.

2. Remove onion and cloves and add the breadcrumbs, which you have made fine by rubbing them through a wire sieve. Simmer sauce gently, stirring continuously, until the breadcrumbs swell and thicken the sauce.

3. Add the butter or cream, and season to taste with salt, white pepper and a pinch of cayenne.

Velouté Sauce (Chicken Velouté)

2 tablespoons butter
2 tablespoons flour
600 ml/1 pint chicken stock
salt
white peppercorns
mushroom peelings or stems
lemon juice

1. Melt butter in the top of a double saucepan, add flour and cook for a few minutes to form pale *roux*. Add boiling stock, salt and peppercorns, and cook, whisking vigorously until well blended.

2. Add mushroom peelings or stems, reduce heat and simmer gently. Stir occasionally and skim from time to time, until the sauce is reduced to

two-thirds of the original quantity and is thick but light and creamy. Flavour with lemon juice and strain through a fine sieve.

Note: This sauce forms the foundation of a number of the best white sauces, which take their distinctive names from the different ingredients added. It can be used by itself, but in that case it is much improved by the addition of a little double cream and egg yolk.

Basic Brown Sauce

2 tablespoons butter
1 small onion, thinly sliced
2 tablespoons flour
750 ml/1¼ pints well-flavoured brown stock
1 small carrot
1 small turnip
1 stick celery or ¼ teaspoon celery seed
4 mushrooms
2-4 tomatoes or 1-2 tablespoons tomato purée
1 bouquet garni (3 sprigs parsley, 1 sprig thyme, 1 bay leaf)
2 cloves
12 black peppercorns
salt

1. Heat butter in a thick-bottomed saucepan until it browns. Add thinly sliced onion and simmer stirring constantly, until golden. Stir in flour and cook, stirring constantly, for a minute longer.

2. The good colour of your sauce depends upon the thorough browning of these ingredients without allowing them to burn. When this is accomplished, remove saucepan from the heat and pour in the stock. Return to heat and stir until it comes to the boil. Allow to boil for 5 minutes, skimming all scum from the top with a perforated spoon.

3. Wash and slice carrot, turnip, celery, mushrooms and tomatoes, and add them with the *bouquet garni*, cloves and peppercorns, and salt, to taste. Simmer the sauce gently for at least 30 minutes, stirring occasionally and skimming when necessary. Strain through a fine sieve, remove fat and reheat before serving.

Brown Chaudfroid Sauce

1 tablespoon gelatine
8 tablespoons cold water
450 ml/¾ pint Basic Brown Sauce (see above)
300 ml/½ pint stock
4-6 tablespoons Madeira or dry sherry

1. Soften gelatine in cold water.

2. Combine Brown Sauce with stock and bring to the boil. Skim well, remove sauce from heat and dissolve gelatine in it. Add Madeira or dry sherry, to taste, and strain sauce through a fine sieve.

Sauce Demi-Glace

600 ml/1 pint Basic Brown Sauce (see above)
chopped stems and peelings of 6 mushrooms
6 tablespoons dry sherry or Madeira
1-2 tablespoons meat glaze

1. Simmer chopped mushroom stems and peelings in dry sherry or Madeira until liquid is reduced by half.

2. Reduce Brown Sauce to half of the original quantity. Then add meat glaze, mushrooms and juices to this mixture, and simmer over a low heat for 15 minutes. Strain before serving.

Basic Court-Bouillon

4.5 litres/8 pints water
150 ml/¼ pint wine vinegar
100 g/4 oz carrots, sliced
100 g/4 oz onions, sliced
1 handful parsley stalks
1 bay leaf
1 sprig thyme
coarse salt
12 peppercorns

1. Combine *Court-Bouillon* ingredients in a large saucepan or fish kettle and bring to the boil; skim and boil for 45 minutes.

2. Strain and cool.

83

Sauce Suprême

84

3 tablespoons butter
2 tablespoons flour
600 ml/1 pint boiling chicken stock
2 button mushrooms, finely chopped
150 ml/¼ pint cream
lemon juice
salt
cayenne

1. Melt 2 tablespoons butter in the top of a double saucepan and blend in the flour thoroughly, being very careful not to let it colour.

2. Remove saucepan from heat and pour in the boiling stock. Cook over water, stirring constantly until it thickens slightly. Add finely chopped mushrooms and simmer for 10 to 15 minutes, stirring from time to time.

3. Strain sauce, reheat and add cream and a little lemon juice. Season to taste with salt and a little cayenne.

4. Remove sauce from the heat and whisk in the remaining butter, adding it in small pieces.
Note: If the sauce is not to be used immediately, put several dabs of butter on top to prevent a skin forming.

Celery Sauce

6 sticks celery, finely sliced
450 ml/¾ pint well-flavoured chicken stock
2 level tablespoons butter
2 level tablespoons flour
150 ml/¼ pint double cream
2 level tablespoons finely chopped parsley
celery salt
freshly ground black pepper
lemon juice

1. Combine finely sliced celery and chicken stock in a saucepan and cook until celery is soft. Keep warm.

2. In the top of a double saucepan, melt butter.

Add flour and cook gently over a low heat, stirring, until *roux* turns a pale golden colour.

3. Add hot celery stock (including celery) and cook over simmering water, stirring occasionally and skimming surface, until sauce has reduced to two-thirds of the original quantity.

4. Stir in double cream; add finely chopped parsley and correct seasoning, adding a little celery salt, freshly ground black pepper and lemon juice, to taste.

Extra-thick White Sauce

butter
½ onion, minced
2 tablespoons flour
300 ml/½ pint hot milk
2 tablespoons lean veal or ham, chopped
1 small sprig thyme
½ bay leaf
white peppercorns
freshly grated nutmeg

1. In a thick-bottomed saucepan, or in the top of a double saucepan, melt 2 tablespoons butter and cook onion in it over a low heat until transparent. Stir in flour and cook for a few minutes, stirring constantly, until mixture cooks through but does not take on colour.

2. Add hot milk and cook, stirring constantly, until the mixture is thick and smooth.

3. In another saucepan, simmer finely chopped lean veal or ham in 1 tablespoon butter over a very low heat. Season with thyme, bay leaf, white peppercorns and grated nutmeg. Cook for 5 minutes, stirring to keep veal from browning.

4. Add veal to the sauce and cook over hot water for 45 minutes to 1 hour, stirring occasionally. When reduced to the proper consistency (two-thirds of the original quantity), strain sauce through a fine sieve into a bowl, pressing meat and onion well to extract all the liquid. Cover surface of sauce with tiny pieces of butter to keep film from forming.

Boiled Chicken with Rice (see page 70)

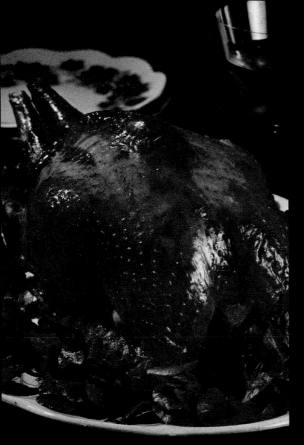
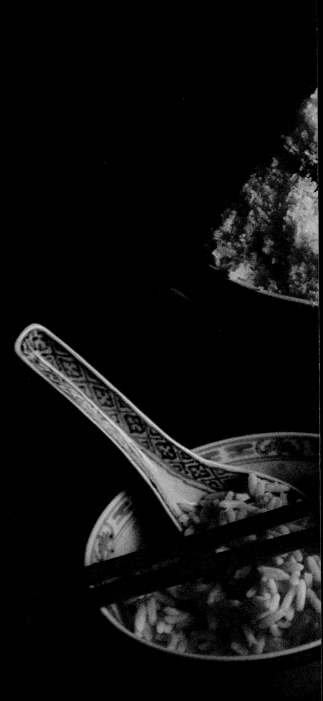

Chicken Stuffed with Grapes (see page 61)
Chicken Baked in Salt (see page 58)

Roast Game Birds

Cream Sauce

3 tablespoons butter
½ onion, minced
2 tablespoons flour
600 ml/1 pint hot milk
2 tablespoons lean veal or ham, chopped
1 small sprig thyme
½ bay leaf
white peppercorns
freshly grated nutmeg
150 ml/¼ pint fresh cream
lemon juice

1. In a thick-bottomed saucepan, or in the top of a double saucepan, melt 2 tablespoons butter and cook onion in it over a low heat until transparent. Stir in flour and cook for a few minutes, stirring constantly, until mixture cooks through but does not take on colour.

2. Add hot milk and cook, stirring constantly, until the mixture is thick and smooth.

3. In another saucepan, simmer finely chopped lean veal or ham in 1 tablespoon butter over a very low heat. Season with thyme, bay leaf, white peppercorns and grated nutmeg. Cook for 5 minutes, stirring to keep veal from browning.

4. Add veal to the sauce and cook over hot water for 45 minutes to 1 hour, stirring occasionally. When reduced to two-thirds of the original quantity, strain sauce through a fine sieve into a bowl, pressing meat and onion well to extract all the liquid. Add fresh cream and a few drops lemon juice. Cover surface of sauce with tiny pieces of butter to keep film from forming.

English Parsley Sauce

1 tablespoon butter
1 tablespoon flour
300 ml/½ pint milk
2 tablespoons finely chopped parsley
salt and white pepper
lemon juice

1. Melt butter in the top of a double saucepan;

stir in the flour and mix with a wooden spoon until smooth. Cook for a few minutes over water but do not allow *roux* to colour.

2. Add milk, heated to boiling point, and cook, stirring constantly, until boiling. Add finely chopped parsley, season to taste with salt and white pepper, and simmer for 2 to 3 minutes longer. Just before serving, add lemon juice, to taste.

Note: A richer sauce can be made by using Béchamel or Velouté Sauce as a foundation.

Béarnaise Sauce

4 sprigs tarragon, chopped
4 sprigs parsley, chopped
1 level tablespoon chopped shallots
2-3 crushed peppercorns
2 tablespoons tarragon vinegar
150 ml/¼ pint dry white wine
3 egg yolks
1 tablespoon water
soft butter, diced
salt
lemon juice
cayenne

1. Reserve 1 level tablespoon each chopped tarragon and parsley, and combine remainder with chopped shallots, crushed peppercorns, vinegar and white wine in the top of a double saucepan. Cook over a high heat until liquid is reduced to approximately 2 tablespoons (practically a glaze). Cool to lukewarm.

2. Beat egg yolks with water and add to the juices in the top of the double saucepan. Stir briskly over hot, but not boiling, water with a wire whisk until light and fluffy. Never let water in bottom of saucepan begin to boil, or sauce will not 'take'.

3. Gradually add butter to egg mixture, whisking briskly as sauce begins to thicken. Continue adding butter and stirring until sauce is thick. Season to taste with salt, lemon juice and cayenne.

4. Strain through a fine sieve, add reserved chopped tarragon leaves and parsley, and serve.

90

Béchamel Sauce

butter
½ onion, minced
2 tablespoons flour
600 ml/1 pint hot milk
2 tablespoons lean veal or ham, chopped
1 small sprig thyme
½ bay leaf
white peppercorns
freshly grated nutmeg

1. In a thick-bottomed saucepan, or in the top of a double saucepan, melt 2 tablespoons butter and cook onion in it over a low heat until transparent. Stir in flour and cook for a few minutes, stirring constantly, until mixture cooks through but does not take on colour.

2. Add hot milk and cook, stirring constantly, until the mixture is thick and smooth.

3. In another saucepan, simmer finely chopped lean veal or ham in 1 tablespoon butter over a very low heat. Season with thyme, bay leaf, white peppercorns and grated nutmeg. Cook for 5 minutes, stirring to keep veal from browning.

4. Add veal to the sauce and cook over hot water for 45 minutes to 1 hour, stirring occasionally. When reduced to the proper consistency (two-thirds of the original quantity), strain sauce through a fine sieve into a bowl, pressing meat and onion well to extract all the liquid. Cover surface of sauce with tiny pieces of butter to keep film from forming.

Note: For a richer Béchamel, remove the saucepan from the heat, add 1 or 2 egg yolks, and heat through. Do not let sauce come to the boil after adding eggs or it will curdle.

French Tomato Sauce

2 tablespoons butter
2 tablespoons finely chopped ham
1 small carrot, finely chopped
1 small turnip, finely chopped
1 onion, finely chopped
1 stick celery, finely chopped
6-8 ripe tomatoes, sliced
2 tablespoons tomato purée
1 tablespoon flour
1 bouquet garni (1 sprig each thyme,
   marjoram and parsley)
300 ml/½ pint well-flavoured beef stock
salt and freshly ground black pepper
lemon juice
sugar

1. Melt butter in a thick-bottomed saucepan, add finely chopped ham and vegetables, and sauté mixture until onion is transparent and soft.

2. Stir in sliced tomatoes and tomato purée, simmer for a minute or two, sprinkle with flour and mix well. Then add *bouquet garni* and beef stock, and simmer gently, stirring continuously, until sauce comes to the boil. Season to taste with salt and freshly ground black pepper, and simmer gently for 30 minutes stirring from time to time. If the sauce becomes too thick, add a little more stock.

3. Strain sauce through a fine sieve, reheat and add lemon juice and sugar, to taste.

Pastry

Puff Pastry (Pâte Feuilletée)

225 g/8 oz plain flour
generous pinch of salt
squeeze of lemon juice
225 g/8 oz butter, finely diced
iced water

1. Sift flour and salt into a clean, dry mixing bowl, and add lemon juice and a quarter of the diced butter. Rub together lightly with the tips of your fingers until the mixture resembles fine breadcrumbs. Then mix with just enough iced water to make a rather stiff dough. Turn on to a floured board and work it well with the hands until it no longer sticks to the fingers and is perfectly smooth. Roll it rather thinly into a square or round shape.

2. The remaining butter to be used should be of the same consistency as the dough, so work it with your hands into a neat thin cake and place it in the centre of the dough. Fold dough up rather loosely, and flatten the folds with a rolling pin. Then roll the pastry into a long narrow strip, being careful not to allow the butter to break through.

3. Fold dough exactly in three, press down the folds and lay the pastry in the refrigerator for at least 15 minutes. This is called giving the pastry one 'turn'; seven of these operations are usually required for puff pastry.

4. The next time the pastry is rolled, place it with the joins at your right-hand side and the open end towards you. Give it two turns this time, and again put it in the refrigerator for at least 15 minutes. Repeat this until the pastry has had seven rolls in all, one roll or 'turn' the first time, and after that two each time with an interval between. The object of cooling the pastry between rolls is to keep the butter and flour in the distinct and separate layers in which the rolling and folding has arranged them. The lightness of your pastry depends upon this. When rolling, keep the pressure of your hands on the rolling pin as even as possible.

5. After you have given the pastry its last roll, put it in the refrigerator for 30 minutes before using it, then roll to the required thickness.

Flaky Pastry

275 g/10 oz plain flour
generous pinch of salt
squeeze of lemon juice
200 g/7 oz butter
iced water

1. Sift flour and salt into a clean, dry bowl and add lemon juice.

2. Divide butter into four equal parts. Take one of these pieces and rub it into the flour with the tips of the fingers until mixture is quite free from lumps. Then add just enough iced water to form dough into one lump. Mix with hands as lightly as possible and turn out on to a floured board. Knead lightly until free from cracks, and then roll out into a long narrow strip, rather less than 5 mm/¼ inch in thickness.

3. Take one of the remaining portions of butter, and with the point of a knife dot it in even rows all over the pastry, leaving a 2.5-cm/1-inch margin without butter round the edges. (If butter is too hard, work it on a plate with a knife before commencing.)

4. Now flour the surface lightly, and fold the pastry exactly in three. Turn the pastry half round, bringing the joins to the right-hand side, and press the folds down sharply with the rolling pin so as to enclose some air.

5. Roll the pastry out again into a long narrow strip, and proceed as before until the two remaining portions of butter have been used. If the butter becomes too soft during the rolling, refrigerate the pastry for a short time before completing the process.

6. The last time, roll the pastry out to the desired thickness, and if it requires widening, turn it across the board and roll across. Never roll in a slanting direction, or the lightness of the pastry will suffer.

Note: This pastry is not quite as rich as puff pastry. Both flaky and puff pastry may be kept for several days in the refrigerator if wrapped in a piece of waxed paper or in a damp cloth.

Index